WAYS OF THE SOUL

The Contemporary Psychology of Ancient Wisdom

Dr Solomon James

Human Assembly Publications

Published by Human Assembly Publications

ISBN-13: 978-1-913816-48-3 (paperback)

Cover Concept: Solomon James & Bernadeta Santo
Cover Design & Book Formatting: Bernadeta Santo

dr.solomonjames@protonmail.com

CONTENTS

Introduction

THE ACORN & THE CATERPILLAR

'Man, we say we know, originates from far away; so far, indeed, that in speaking of his origin, such phrases as "beyond the stars" are frequently employed. Man is estranged from his origins. Some of his feelings (but not all of them) are slight indicators of this…Man has the opportunity of returning to his origins. He has forgotten this. He is, in fact, "asleep" to the reality.'

Ustad Hilmi, Mevlevi ('Thinkers of the East')

Overall, people tend to be unhappy not because of what they know but because of what they don't know. In other words, personal fulfilment is about having a connection to something that is *beyond* us.

We are currently living in an age of separation, and this disconnection is at the root of many of our social ills. Broadly speaking, humanity is in crisis - individually, collectively, and at a deep 'soulful' level. It is a crisis of the inner self, and society reflects these fractures. This longing of reunion, reconnection (however we wish to name it) has been at the core of a developmental impulse through the ages. It has also manifested within many genuine 'spiritual' traditions and forms that arose to answer this need. Yet much was lost along the way. The road of deep connection, of essential communion between Self and Source, is never easy nor automatic. It must be sought. A good doctor does not offer a cure without first understanding the cause of what ills the patient. A good doctor also knows that the patient carries the potential for the cure within them.

Everything in life is in process. Nothing is static and all things, all life, is in movement. Yet there are different ways in which this movement can operate. It can be gradual, suppressed, or it can be accelerated. Let us take the analogy of the acorn and the caterpillar. The acorn, as we know, carries within it all the information it requires to grow into an oak tree. What it requires from the outside is time and favourable environmental conditions. With these it can gradually, over many generations, grow up from the acorn in the soil to the grand oak tree that reaches for the sky. This is a gradual process that moves along a natural rhythm. We can say that this represents the general path of natural development. Then there is the caterpillar.

The caterpillar also contains within it all the information it needs for its future growth. It may not be fully aware of this, yet if it follows its instinct it will come to a point in its life where it feels the need to make a change. It will enter into the cocoon state and, if internal conditions are favourable, it will eventually emerge into a butterfly. That is, it will undergo a radical transformation into something new. It will not be an extension of its old self, like the oak tree is to the acorn; but will transform into a new state of being - *if internal conditions are favourable.*

What this analogy tells us is that there is gradual evolutionary growth as well as rapid, evolutionary transformations. As it is with the caterpillar, so it can be with humankind. We can choose to be recipients of environmental conditions that favour our gradual development over generations. Or we can make a conscious, concerted effort to utilize internal conditions to trigger a rapid, and radical, transformation of our being.

Buckminster Fuller once said that 'There is nothing in a caterpillar that tells you it's going to be a butterfly.' The outward signs are not readily distinguishable. There are no neon signs announcing the capacity for transformation within. Yet it exists. The program for *transcending ourselves* is written into our code. What is required to unlock this code is correct intention.

In its essence, this is what this short book discusses.

This book refers to a perennial psychology in terms of a developmental path. That is, it symbolizes a transcendental urge to live with principles and aims that are beyond ordinary life. To live 'beyond' ordinary life whilst simultaneously participating in daily life is the axiom of the perennial psychology. To be 'of the world' and yet 'not of the world' represents a long existing tradition that has operated – and continues to operate – within all cultures and all times throughout human civilization. It may be that, in its essence, the purpose of humankind is a transformational one.

A genuine perennial psychology recognizes that human life is constantly under the impacts of what can be termed as 'developmental forces.' These forces can assist in advancing human cognition and perception. And that without these impulses permeating our lives, humanity simply would not exist in its current state. It is what makes the very fabric of our existence, yet we seldom recognize its presence. We are more likely to recognize, and have contact, only with its remnants or decayed forms. The perennial psychology has, at all times, existed to assist in the 'refinement' of the human being to perceive this impulse. This correspondence must be an active and conscious process for it requires that a person lessens the influence of life's constant distractions.

The perennial psychology has as its principal objectives the aim to a) reveal to us who we truly are; and b) to assist us to develop our inner cognition. This path has been at the heart of all genuine religious-spiritual impulses at their birth, before they decayed into secondary accretions. In essence, the perennial psychology is 'truth without form.' However, in order for its wisdom to be delivered in a contemporary form for its receiving culture, it must find a suitable vehicle or channel. This book discusses some of this wisdom and its various contemporary forms.

Now that we have entered the twenty-first century we are especially in need of a modern recognition of this ancient and perennial path. It appears as if in recent times we have become bankrupt in the stories we tell ourselves. Much of modern life is in dissonance. We are in need of more magical stories so that we may once again recognize and incorporate the metaphysical background of the world. Humanity is in danger of losing its identity as a precious, noble species. It seems that we may have lost some of our passion and commitment to life and its mystery. Some people in the modern world are already living in a state of 'reality apathy.' The external world feeds us with false stories that distract us from the essential. We need to take a step back and to find our own individual stories. Humanity came here long ago and has lost its way. As the Persian poet Jalaluddin Rumi said -

Whoever brought me here will have to take me back:
All day I think about it, then at night I say it.

Where did I come from and what am I supposed to be doing?
I have no idea.
My soul is from elsewhere, I'm sure of that,
and I intend to end up there.

This drunkenness began in some other tavern.
When I get back around to that place,
I'll be completely sober. Meanwhile,
I'm like a bird from another continent, sitting in this aviary.
The day is coming when I fly off,
But who is it now in my ear, who hears my voice?
Who says words with my mouth?

Who looks out with my eyes? What is the soul?
I cannot stop asking.
If I could taste one sip of an answer,
I could break out of this prison for drunks.
I didn't come here of my own accord,
and I can't leave that way.
Whoever brought me here will have to take me back.[1]

We are in search of our soulful connection - to find our way back home. First, we need to recognize that a path exists.

References

[1] Barks Coleman, Moyne John (trans). 1996. *The Essential Rumi.* New York: HarperCollins, p2

Chapter One

SOUL-MAKING

'There is one thing in this world which must never be forgotten. If you were to forget everything else, but did not forget that, then there would be no cause to worry; whereas if you performed and remembered and did not forget every single thing, but forget that one thing, then you would have done nothing whatsoever. It is just as if a king had sent you to the country to carry out a specified task. You go and perform a hundred other tasks; but if you have not performed that particular task on account of which you had gone to the country, it is as though you have performed nothing at all. So man has come in this world for a particular task, and that is his purpose; if he does not perform it, then he will have done nothing.'

Rumi

Humanity did not come here for nothing. When our early cave-dwelling ancestors first made their handprints upon the rock walls they were making a statement, an expression, of their presence. They were signalling to the world around them that 'I am here – I exist. We are human.' It was a statement also of intent. This show of presence was a declaration that 'they' knew they were here – in this world, in this reality. And it marked the beginning of a long journey to come home.

It is said in the wisdom traditions that human beings are ordinarily cut off from Objective Reality, which is the true origin of everything. As Plato would say, the human being is separated from the true realm of Forms. Due to this disconnection our human perceptions are limited and are only capable of receiving upon a much-restricted wavelength. We perceive as if through a thin slit and we are unable to grasp the bigger picture. The result of this is that we perceive secondary effects and consider them to be primary. It is like seeing the leaves of a tree sway in the wind and thinking that the leaves are themselves the cause of their movement. We are unable to see beyond – to perceive the wind that blows. We are conditioned to see the caused and not to perceive there is a causer.

There is a phrase that says – 'The colour of the water seems to be the colour of the glass into which it has been poured.'

It is also said that there are three kinds of men and women. The first are totally animal, and they live an ordinary life. In this category are included most people – the regular thinkers and philosophers, emotional religionists, the everyday person, and all those who do not really know that they exist. The second kind of people are those who, even in ordinary life, have acquired permanency. They live on two planes, that of ordinary existence and another one. The third category are those who exist on three planes and have no limit in time. The object of human existence on earth is to develop within the permanency of the second and third conditions.

Humankind has had the possibility for conscious development for many thousands of years. Largely this potential has been woefully underused.

In the tradition of the Kabbalah there is the concept of *tikkun*, which refers to the idea that everyone is placed here on Earth to fulfil a particular mission. As an ancient Hasidic aphorism states, it is 'a task that belongs to no other.' Many traditions speak of being in exile from our origins – the Source of All (SoA). We are constantly encouraged to strive for a return to remembrance and closeness to our original Source. The early Kabbalistic text *Bahir* notes that 'People want to see the King, but do not know where to find his house. First, they [must] ask, "Where is the King's house?" Only then can they ask, "Where is the King?"'[1]

Similarly, the Gnostic tradition speaks of the precious jewel -

In a remote realm of perfection, there was a just monarch who had a wife and a wonderful son and daughter. They all lived together in happiness.

One day the father called his children before him and said:

'The time has come, as it does for all. You are to go down, an infinite distance, to another land. You shall seek and find and bring back a precious Jewel.'

The travellers were conducted in disguise to a strange land, whose inhabitants almost all lived a dark existence. Such was the effect of this place that the two lost touch with each other, wandering as if asleep.

From time to time they saw phantoms, similitudes of their country and of the Jewel, but such was their condition that these things only increased the depth of their reveries, which they now began to take as reality.

When news of his children's plight reached the king, he sent word by a trusted servant, a wise man:

'Remember your mission, awaken from your dream, and remain together.'

With this message they roused themselves, and with the help of their rescuing guide they dared the monstrous perils which surrounded the Jewel, and by its magic aid returned to their realm of light, there to remain in increased happiness for evermore.[2]

A known dervish phrase says that: life is a gift that consists of three days and two are gone. The reader should keep in mind that all who come into this existence will also have to leave it. No one stays forever. There are those who came before us, and those who will come after. Life is a transitory thing. And with every breath our stay here decreases.

It says in the Zohar that 'Man, whilst in this world, considers not and reflects not what he is standing on, and each day as it passes, he regards as though it has vanished into nothingness.'[3] We seek after self-renewal, yet we recognize it not. Each person yearns for something deep, yet this is often ignored or misread into different needs and desires.

Each person carries within them the potential for visionary inspiration. This is often blocked, discouraged, or ignored through our social conditioning. A person may feel a little silly these days in admitting that they long for an invisible, immaterial, and intransient thing. We often substitute with false words, surrendering to the consensus attitudes prevalent in our cultures. Our religious buildings and institutions are in disarray and decay – both outwardly and inwardly. The 'temple of union' is in need of being reinforced to its original state – within the heart of humankind. The revered connection between each person and the Source-of-All lies within each self. We are each the meeting point of union between the material and the Source. In this world – in this reality – we are given responsibility to connect the transcendent with the everyday. This is what is meant by the term 'soul-making.'

Today, the search for truth for many people has become a cliché, a result of ennui, or a commercial industry. Rarely do we find it stripped down to its essential bare bones. The human being is largely self-blinded. We have not learnt how to read or speak our own inner language. The French writer Voltaire wrote that – *'Four thousand volumes of metaphysics will not teach us what the soul is.'* We can only learn by living it.

In this life, we live but once. We give effort to learn and gain expertise about things in the outer world, yet rarely do we aim to master ourselves. Our knowledge of the physical world is great whilst that of the inner world of the human being is lacking. The fundamental nature of the human being has not changed over the many millennia of our human history. What has changed is our social milieu and our means and ways of expression. *How* we understand has changed – not *what* there is to understand. The plain fact is that we have forgotten who we truly are. We live our lives as personalities. These personalities are created through social systems and become our masks. Finally, they become who we think we are. We spend a lifetime living within our masks. The human being walks through the roads of life as if through foreign lands. We are losing our centre of being – losing contact with our core essential groundedness. Fundamentally, at core, the human is a developmental being.

Few people ever stop to question the issue of selfhood – who really am I? What does it truly mean to have an 'I'? Surely, we cannot be body and mind alone? Are we to believe that our existence is the result of accidental evolution and our minds are the accidental result from random neuronal pathways? Are we really this blind? Rabbi Israel Salanter said that: 'Man lives with himself for seventy years, but does not get to know himself.' In our essential selves there exist unknown and unimaginable capacities. And yet we so often behave like a drunken person who has no idea about their drunkenness. They are drunk. They cannot perceive what lays beyond their inebriated state. The average 'drunken' person thinks in set patterns and cannot easily adjust themselves to a different cognitive reality.

A person largely lies hidden beneath their tongue. We present ourselves through our words. We should treat our words as if they were our children. They are born from us and go forth from us. They are the little 'I's' and 'me's' that we send into the world; too often we send them out blackened. We do not realize that our words are tied to us if by a golden thread. When we release our words, we are releasing those things that dwell within us. At all times we are weaving the golden thread; it is unfortunate that far too often this thread is cast like a net of iron. There is a line of communication with the heart-self, and it is through this we are compelled to learn how to speak. We are first bound to acquire a new way of looking at things. The necessary training is to develop new senses of perception that are timeless. The task that lies ahead is to develop advanced human cognition. This can be said to also be a part of the soul-making process, and it occurs in everyday life.

Soul-making, as well as taking care of one's soul, are not specifically introverted or monastic pursuits. They do not require steadfast introspection or withdrawal from the world. In some moments perhaps, yet not as part of their continual pursuit. The Romantic Poet Keats said – 'Call the world if you please, "the vale of Soul-making." Then you will find out the use of the world.' The use of the world is to help us develop our capacities for re-connection with Source.

We have developed our faith, our reason, our mental pursuits; we have established industry and created marvellous technologies – yet we have failed to work on ourselves. We have largely ignored to develop our cognitive capacities. The connection with Source is an inoculation against the ills of the world; against the negative impacts and influences. It is like an inner medicine against the worldly disease. What can be called as 'soul-making,' or perceptive cognition, needs to be re-imagined and reintegrated into our lives. This is not about going back to animism or alchemy. The necessary stimulus can be found here, in the everyday world around us. It is also a part of the world, our extended reality. The alchemist Sendivogius said – 'The greater part of the soul lies outside the body.'

It is often assumed that something transcendental must be far off or complicated. This is ignorance, or a lazy excuse. Such things are only 'far off' in a direction people don't comprehend or wish to look. It is an assumption to think that reality makes itself visible to us in ordinary life. We would do well to consider that genuine 'Reality' is actually invisible in our lives until we make it visible. The ancient wisdom traditions sought to make the Truth visible within the semi-visible reality of everyday life. In the ordinary perception of reality, the Truth is nowhere visible yet everywhere present. It works undisclosed in spite of ourselves. Truth works to transform life, as well as it is a human function to convert Truth into life. Such Truth is not occult theatrics – it is extraordinary and beyond normal comprehension. And no gold in the world can ever buy it.

In this respect, the world and Nature is our monastery; and life can also be our teacher. The Path of soul-making is about seeking for fishes of gold within the material rivers of sand. If we can walk through life with our hearts awake (perceptive cognition), then our lives will change. Time is needed for a tree to bear fruit. Likewise, the human being requires time, effort, and correct intention to bear its own precious fruit. The human tree requires the longest time of any fruit tree. For this, patience and perseverance are required. Sources of nourishment must be continually sought.

It is said that the human being always moves from one state of nourishment to the next. As an embryo, our nourishment was once blood. Then as young babies it changed to milk. At some point we were weaned onto solid food. For most people, solid food shall remain their continual source of nourishment. Yet there will be some people who will shift from solid food to a different kind of nourishment - a less physical and visible one. It is these people who seek for soul-making. Life is a state of being weaned from one type of nourishment to another. We may also be weaned from the visible to the non-visible. It is well to remember that the human being belongs to a royal lineage even though it may appear that they are dressed in rags.

The path of the perennial psychology is not for everyone. Not everyone will feel drawn to this endeavour. Yet whoever puts themselves right within will put their whole life right. The essential is the beginning. And everything begins and ends at the beginning. These are the places where the wise streams flow.

I wish to arrive at the beginning with a story. It is the story of 'The Forbidden Room:'

> *'Once upon a time there was a young man who decided to go in search of work. He walked down the street, and as he was passing a magnificent palace an old man came out and asked if by any chance he was looking for work. The young man accepted the offer and soon went to work in the palace where he found that it was inhabited by ten old men.*
>
> *As time went by, the old men died until there was only one*

left alive. He said to the young man: "You will shortly inherit this whole palace, as there is no other heir. I would just warn you of one thing; and that is never to open this door here – not under any circumstances. As for the rest, you may do as you like."

For a time, the young man heeded the advice. Eventually, however, he began to reason that if the palace belonged to him then surely there could be no good cause for him not to look where he liked. Also, that there was surely nothing so horrible he could not contemplate it.

So the young man opened the door, and there he saw a long corridor. He walked down it and when he came to the end he looked around and found that the corridor had disappeared. He found himself on a desolate seashore; and as he was wondering what to do he heard the sound of beating wings and looked up to see a giant bird swooping down on him. The bird picked him up in its talons and carried him off across the sea to a far-off land. There it set him down on the turret of a castle.

The castle belonged to a King whose daughter fell in love with the new arrival. Soon they were married, and the young man settled down to a prosperous life. One day the King's daughter said to him: "Half of all that I have is yours. However, there is one condition, and that is that under no circumstances must you ever open this door here, as the consequences will be extremely serious." For a time the young man heeded this advice, until one day he thought to himself that since he shared everything with his wife, what possible reason could she have for hiding something from him? So when next alone he opened the door, and went down the corridor he found beyond. And when he got to the end he found himself in exactly the same place and situation as he had been in before the old man had asked him to work in the palace. He had no recollection of the events which had befallen him, and the only thing which remained was an everlasting sense of loss.'

References

[1]Hoffman, Edward. 1996. *The Heavenly Ladder: Kabbalistic Techniques for Inner Growth.* Sturminster Newton: Prism Press, p20

[2]Shah, I. 1971. *Thinkers of the East.* London: Jonathan Cape, p123

[3]Hoffman, Edward. 1996. *The Heavenly Ladder: Kabbalistic Techniques for Inner Growth.* Sturminster Newton: Prism Press, p23

Chapter Two

WISE STREAMS FLOW

'To all of us falls one heritage - Wisdom. All of us inherit of it equally. But one man makes the best of his heritage, and another does not; one buries it, lets it die, and passes over it; another draws profit from it — one more, one less. According to how we invest, use, and administer our heritage, we obtain much or little from it; and yet it belongs to all of us, and it is in all of us.'

Paracelsus

Throughout the ages various wisdom streams (teachings) have operated within humanity with the aim and intention of permanently raising the consciousness (cognition) of a person/group/community to a 'higher' – or finer – level of perception. When a permanent state has been achieved, the individual and/or group is able to operate within one of several realms which are perceived through this newly restored capacity. Temporary glimpses of these realms are what have fascinated humankind for eons, stretching as far back as when our human ancestors were cave dwellers. Such glimpses have also come through the long history of shamanism; as well as spiritual trances; religious rituals; and the inculcation of ecstatic states, etc. For as long as humanity has existed, it has been experiencing glimpses of other realms, and thereby attempting, through many and various means, to recapture these experiences. These are, and continue to be, the doorways into the multi-dimensional realms.

Less well known is the knowledge that the key to these multi-dimensional doorways lie within the very heart of ourselves. In the past these internal codes required specialist training and knowledge to access and to activate them. This is the history of some of the long trials and discipline of a spiritual/developmental path. Alternatively, they were accidentally and temporarily glimpsed through such events as a near-death experience, shock, or similar impact.

There can be a seemingly random contact achieved between ordinary life and the non-material realms. These contacts have sometimes been glimpsed – in a transitory manner – by the use of 'artificial aids,' such as by means of intoxication (biologically and/or chemically influenced). Many people have attempted to recapture these transitory experiences, incorrectly thinking or believing that it will lead to a permanent state. This activity, and this way of thinking, is more destructive than good. What this shows is a lack of perception on the part of the individual; an accumulation of incorrect information. This reveals itself by a person attempting to induce such transitory experiences when they clearly lack the knowledge of how to correctly learn from and utilize their experience. Without a correct developmental function, such experiences more than not serve to destabilize, or to confuse the person at best.

However, such glimpses into the other realms show us that the state of the Real is timeless. Jesus, in the apocryphal Gospel of Mary, is noted as saying 'Be above time.' That is, to be connected to a supratemporal state. At the same time, it is necessary to learn how to function correctly within the realm of current reality. And this is the crux: to function as harmonious, balanced, and constructive members of society whilst also perceiving and operating through an objective Reality. To be both within *our times* as well as within the *timeless*. This is the matter at hand that faces the modern seeker. The perennial psychology reflects this because although it operates within our times it is essentially timeless.

Many ancient tales, fables, allegories, etc, are representations of what we refer to as a 'higher dimension' operating within our own. As these *interventions* become more frequent and noticeable, we begin to question the current paradigm of reality. Eventually a stage is reached whereby such 'anomalies' are so prevalent that a person is compelled to re-evaluate and finally modify their consensus of reality. What we generally take to be reality is in fact a distortion, and only part of the 'bigger picture.' It can be said that humanity is now collectively at the stage whereby it needs to modify the consensus understanding of reality. This is now critical.

According to both Kabbalah and Jewish philosophy, it is the responsibility of humanity to 'repair the world' – to engage in the process of *tikkun olam*. The perennial psychology has worked with, and through, individuals in order to assist in 'repairing the world' by first elevating the perceptions of the few. It is important to stress here that the first task is to elevate the perceptions of those who are to take the responsibility for assisting to improve worldly conditions. Otherwise, mixed results are liable to occur. Needless to say, only a very few in each age have taken up the offer of wisdom. As it is said in Proverbs: 'I have called, and ye refused; I have stretched out my hand, and no man regardeth' (Prov. 1:20, 24). The doors of the sanctuary are ajar. They have always been open in every culture, in every epoch. As it is said,

The knowledge of God cannot be attained by seeking, but only those who seek it find it.

Bastami

The path of the primordial, perennial wisdom has always existed. From the earliest Oracles of the Mystery Traditions (Chaldean and Orphic) to the initiatory streams within the Abrahamic religions. The lineage was kept alive by certain schools or 'impulses' of wisdom – by Neoplatonic and Sufic streams operative in the Middle East, Europe and elsewhere; in Kabbalah through teachings of correspondences; the Hermetic sciences; the science of Alchemy; Gnostic elements in Christianity; as well as numerous known and unknown Orders, societies, and groups. The wisdom stream flows also through each civilization and culture according to its specific mode of transmission.

At a brief glance it is seen that Hermetic, Neoplatonic, and Gnostic works of literature were produced in the first three centuries A.D. during the height of Roman Empire. This was a time where globalization, urbanization, and multiculturalism were replacing older traditions and simpler faiths. Civilizations and cultures have their unique essences, often characterized in its monuments, institutions, and their ways of communicating ideas. For example, the Roman civilization had their public works, roads, aqueducts, amphitheatres, etc. They had institutions of law, order, military, administration. They transmitted ideas through literature and law and order. The Mediaeval Christian civilization had their great cathedral monuments, the ecclesiastical institution; and transmission of ideas through religion and ritual. In this age ideas were spread through astrology, alchemy and Kabbalah, as well as an interest in various occult practices.

Similarly, the European Renaissance emerged in Western cities at the same time when economic and cultural progress were taking over from a waning tide of medieval beliefs. The Renaissance culture had their universities as monuments, humanism as an institution, and transmitted ideas through art and literature. Whereas the arts today are seen largely in terms of entertainment, their original purpose was in civilizing humanity through the deliberate use of highly developed techniques and tools.

Europe experienced another stream of operations in the late nineteenth century as it entered a period of sustained urban and industrial growth. With the rise of scientism and secularism came a decline in organized religion. Around this time arrived a resurgence in occultism and esoteric societies alongside a modern-day theosophy, such as in Madame Blavatsky and ceremonial magic. The Western streams witnessed the figures of such 20th century esotericists as Rudolf Steiner, Alice Bailey, and G. I. Gurdjieff. This later merged with the rise of depth psychology (Carl Jung), and then with transcendental psychology in the second half of the century. These transmissions were also blighted by the rise of a modern western capitalist consumer culture that birthed the New Age movement, guruism, self-help, life coaching, and commercial self-development practices. However, the genuine perennial psychology has no central institution, no standard curriculum, and no permanent residence. As the Persian poet-mystic Rumi says:

'I am not of the East, nor of the West;
Not of the land, not of the sea;
Neither of this world, nor of the next;
My place is placeless, my trace traceless.'

It is not a combination of different faiths but is a specific kind of inner knowledge that can be projected and seeded into a culture. It can also be transmitted to an individual who has undergone a certain amount of preparation (more on this later).

Ideas are seeded in different ways depending on the culture. It could be through religious ideas, philosophy, psychology, art, charity, law and order, and certain individuals who represent these streams. The ways and means all serve to develop culture, civilization, and ultimately humanity. It can be said that they work to 'feed the soul' of the culture. History is a vast tapestry in which each person, community, nation, and civilization has a role to play. Those people at a lower state of awareness are subject to the general sway of conditions and influences, be they good or bad.

At a general level of awareness there is no perceptible pattern to events. We neither see nor intuit any over-arching grand design. This is because we do not have access to objective reality or advanced cognition. Some people believe that there is no longer a perennial wisdom lineage and that the seeker must find their developmental path through their own solitary efforts. This belief is incorrect. Whilst individual efforts are necessary, at some point assistance – or an *intervention* – is required. The genuine seeker shall receive a response.

The perennial psychology belongs to all ages and all times. It is neither time-bound nor culture-restricted. It is a living stream of knowledge that adopts to the time, place, and people within which it operates. It has been, and continues to be, a guide that illumines the way home. In past epochs the perennial psychology – or wisdom tradition, as it was often referred to – was a body of knowledge that was the closely guarded property of initiates. Today, there is much knowledge freely available to us without fear of being executed for heresy! In present times it can be said that this knowledge exists as an open secret. It only appears invisible or closed because of one's own blindness, or social conditionings. Whilst it has not always operated openly in society, its presence has existed through objects, buildings, groupings, events, etc, as well as written texts. Most often it functions in ways people are not aware of, and in ways not expected. Yet it has always been available, and often it has quite literally been right in front of our eyes. Currently, another stage of its operation has been arrived at. That is why this book has been written.

The wisdom stream is now visible in our western cultures in a way like never before. It's texts and ideas have become a part of popular culture, unbeknown to most of us. Its signs can be found within both adult and children's entertainment, disseminated through an array of channels. The diffusion today exists at an unprecedented level. It is now a part of our present cultural consciousness - only that *we* may not recognize this consciously. Modern science is also discovering a new understanding of how reality operates, similar to what has been known to the wisdom stream for millennia. As one example, recent quantum field theories describe manifest reality in terms of universal interconnectedness; this interpretation reflects the long-known wisdom of correspondence. The sciences are also now suggesting a reciprocity, or intercommunication, between the human being and the fundamental 'reality field.' Knowledge long held is now being known through other means and entering our modern understanding of the world.

The perennial psychology belongs to all times, as at its heart it is a science of the human being. As such, it sits comfortably within our contemporary times, and can relate to the new discoveries in science, cosmology, consciousness, and psychology. No part of human knowledge is outside the remit of a genuine path of perennial psychology. What it represents is an objective body of knowledge, and its transmission. It is not a religion, a cult, or a system of belief. Neither is it specifically a 'spiritual' path. It is an exact science that leads to the advancement of human cognition and perception that develops a higher understanding and knowledge. The transmission also corresponds to a capacity inherent within humanity – a level of development that would surprise most people.

The idea of human development is well-known and accepted in western societies largely because there is a strong emphasis upon the individual and on the individual's relationship with their grasp of reality. Partly because of this, the Western wisdom traditions have emphasized the use of the imagination and psychological tools for developing and refining human perception.

It is often the case that a resurgence in such ideas as self-development often occur when there is a backlash or retreat away from orthodox belief systems. When cultural institutions are shown to be lacking and unable to offer any real nourishment, there is an openness to alternative paths. It should also be noted that previous wisdom traditions may no longer be functioning as active transmissions of the higher knowledge. Everything in this dense material reality succumbs to the same laws of decay and crystallization (i.e., loss of kinetic energy). It can be surmised that at present there is a concentrated effort to transmit the wisdom tradition in a scientific-psychological context for the 21st

century. For this reason, I have chosen to refer to the ancient wisdom tradition as the perennial psychology.

The perennial psychology can be referred to as a path of gnosis. True gnosis (not the intellectual concept) is a cognitive insight that is perceived through direct experience. It can only be taught to a limited degree. After that, direct experience is essential. Gnosis is the act of objective understanding whilst *dia*gnosis is the secondary act of rational examination. Modern societies have placed diagnosis as the principle form of attaining knowledge at the expense of the genuine insights of gnosis. True gnosis is an objective developmentary impulse that sustains our material world. This knowledge, and the people who operate according to it, are engaged in an evolutionary activity. This primordial wisdom evolves within people, and by engaging with it, people are aided in their personal evolution. The timing of certain activities along the perennial path follows a very clear pattern, which is beyond most people's capacity to comprehend. Here is a short story to illustrate this:

> *'Unjustly imprisoned, a tinsmith was allowed to receive a rug woven by his wife. He prostrated himself upon the rug day after day to say his prayers, and after some time he said to his jailers:*
>
> *"I am poor and without hope, and you are wretchedly paid. But I am a tinsmith. Bring my tin and tools and I shall make small artifacts which you can sell in the market, and we will both benefit."*

The guards agreed to this, and presently the tinsmith and they were both making a profit, from which they bought food and comfort for themselves. Then, one day, when the guards went to the cell, the door was open, and he was gone.

Many years later, when this man's innocence had been established, the man who had imprisoned him asked him how he had escaped, what magic he had used. He said:

"It is a matter of design, and design within design. My wife is a weaver. She found the man who had made the locks of the cell door, and got the design from him. This she wove into the carpet, at the spot where my head touched in prayer five times a day. I am a metal-worker, and this design looked to me like the inside of a lock. I designed the plan of the artifacts to obtain the materials to make the key - and I escaped."'

It is possible, within the captivity of our contemporary lives, to escape the program of our conditioning.

In human culture and society there are people of destiny. These are the people who choose to develop their full capacity as human beings. First, such people are required to become what are called *seekers*. At a certain stage each seeker will need assistance from a teacher (one who has travelled the path before). Such teachers may or may not present themselves physically within a person's lifetime. The function of the teacher is to prepare a seeker so that they are able to recognize their capacity. To begin with, the seeker must understand how much of their ordinary thinking is restricted by social conditioning. Until this point is reached, true understanding is impossible, and the seeker is only suitable for one or another of the more usual human organizations that operate along rigid social norms.

It has already been said that we have become disconnected from our Source. The perennial psychology reminds us of this, and the separation from our true home. As Rumi says:

> 1. Listen to this reed how it complains:
> it is telling a tale of separations.
> 2. Saying, "Ever since I was parted from the reed-bed,
> man and woman have moaned in (unison with) my lament.
> 3. I want a bosom torn by severance,
> that I may unfold (to such a one) the pain of love-desire.
> 4. Every one who is left far from his source
> wishes back the time when he was united with it."[1]

Similarly, Jesus is quoted as saying: 'The foxes have their holes and the birds have nests, but the son of man has nowhere to rest his head' (Matthew 8:20). The human being has no real home in this world. To begin the journey home will cost us all that we have.

The poet T.S. Eliot wrote that the price of love is 'Costing not less than everything' – this is also the price of truth. It is a price that cannot be wasted. Here is a story:

A wise Queen gazed out over her kingdom. She was content knowing that she had dedicated her life in service to her land and its people. The kingdom had grown into stability and harmony. Yet the Queen was concerned that perhaps some of the people had become complacent. She decided that she would announce a competition. She would give a bag of gold to the person who could demonstrate the most unusual thing.

Word soon spread over the kingdom and in the coming weeks people came from near and far to the Queen's court in order to show off their 'unusual thing.' There were people who walked on hands or danced in the most strangest of ways. One person played like a flute through their fluttering fingers. Another sang like a nightingale whilst another warbled like a mockingbird. The Queen enjoyed the show, yet nothing came close to being the most unusual.

Finally, one day an old man entered the court and claimed that he could thread a needle from 30 meters. The Queen raised her eyebrows in disbelief. If the old man could surely achieve this, then it would indeed be the most unusual thing. Accordingly, the old man was allowed entry into one of the towers of the courtyard. Below a high window 30 meters up the old man positioned himself carefully. Down within the courtyard at the base of the tower stood a lady of the Queen's court with a silver needle in her fingers. After a long time of waiting the old man eventually released his thread. Slowly it fell to the ground and, to everyone's astonishment, it fell directly through the eye of the needle. The court was amazed and cheered the old man.

As soon as the old man had come down the tower the Queen presented him with his reward – a bag full of gold. 'Tell me,' said the Queen. 'How did you achieve this most unusual feat?'

'Highness,' replied the old man somewhat proudly, 'I have been practicing this all my life. I have climbed high trees for over fifty years and each day I practiced.

'And your family? Your job?' enquired the Queen.

The old man shook his head. 'I was too busy practicing threading the needle to be concerned with such things. Yet finally I did it,' said the man with a smile. 'And now I am rich because of it.'

The Queen immediately grabbed the bag of gold away from the old man. 'You were rewarded the bag of gold for your unusual feat. Now I am punishing you for having wasted your life.'

And the Queen had the old man sent away never to be seen again.

References

[1]*The Song of the Reed* (Masnavi, Book 1: Lines 1-34). Translation by Nicholson, 1926

Chapter Three

THROUGH THE LOOKING GLASS

"I saw a child carrying a light.
I asked him where he had brought it from.
He put it out and said:
'Now you tell me where it is gone.'"
Hasan of Basra

The perennial psychology provides a path to a deeper truth, to a more expansive perceptive capacity, without disturbing a person's equilibrium or their ability to lead normal, social lives. Often, so-called developmental paths have led to anti-social individuals or those who 'drop out' of their social responsibilities. On the contrary, any genuine path refines a person's ability to deal with their regular social lives. Any conflict between a person and their society/community is a mark of a corrupted teaching.

A Sufi master once said: 'If ordinary people, who admit the imperfection of their knowledge, can sustain society, how much more can the Sufi manage to retain his equilibrium, faced both with the principles of the environment and the knowledge of where it fits in with an Ultimate Reality.' The perennial psychology has operated throughout all times, and under various names. However, it is a common trait that people often get caught up in attachment to names. If I mention a Sufi master, is the perennial psychology therefore a Sufi path? Or if I quote from the Kabbalah or Jewish philosophy is it an 'esoteric' part of Judaism? Meister Eckhart said, 'If you haven't the truth of which we are speaking in yourselves, you cannot understand me.' By quoting from Eckhart, is the path Christian mysticism? It is all and yet none of these. As Eckhart said, each person needs to contact the truth within themselves in order to understand beyond the externals. The crux of the matter is our capacity to perceive, which is a function of cognition. Perception is that which releases as well as that which binds us. It can be our liberator as well as our jailer. We often fail to realize that what we take to be our experience of the world is a result of the limits of our perception.

As a young boy I had, like many other children, a telescope in which to look at the stars at night. I would look through this basic telescope to observe the pinpoints of starlight within the dark canopy of space. I remember being awed by the small offerings the telescope provided. I used to think of those big telescopes that professional astronomers use to observe the workings of our known universe. Then the question arose: humans invented and created the telescope. It is designed to correlate with human vision. The more sophisticated telescopes use high-definition lenses that have still been designed by human minds. What we are able to see, and the data we receive, corresponds to the human biological system. So, are we seeing *what is actually there* or are we receiving data according to *our perceptive capability?* Would another sentient species perceive an altogether different awareness of the universe? In fact, a different species may be operating on an altogether different dimensional wavelength. We understand our universe, and we speculate about our role in the cosmos, according to our status as human beings. We are consigned to the perceptive range accorded to the standard operating human nervous system. What if the human nervous system were to be adapted to perceive differently?

As human beings, we relate to reality through the looking glass of the human body. Furthermore, the senses through which we operate are influenced by our social and cultural contexts. This process of social conditioning reflects greatly in how we come to regard the external world. Our beliefs, opinions, emotions, and thought processes are a culmination of complex layers of environmental conditioning. Most educated people can comprehend this and will agree to it. However, what it less known about is our dimensional conditioning. That is, those limitations placed on us through our perceptive faculties. A genuine developmental path seeks to work at deconditioning a person from social-cultural layering as well as from perceptive limitations.

Universal phenomenon, and the working of physical laws, are known to us according to the measurements that operate within our dimension. The human senses perceive only a very thin slither of the full visible spectrum. Not only does the non-visible spectrum exist (some of which can be detected through our instruments) but also there are elements within our dimension that are not known to us. Then, also, there are phenomena existing beyond our known dimension. Overall, it can be said that the human being has access to only a very small portion of phenomena. Human perception of known reality is extremely limited, to say the least. And from this very limited information we make up our knowledge base of the world and the cosmos. From this knowledge base we then construct our views and understanding of human life and the meaning of existence. There are ways, however, of widening this understanding by expanding human cognition and perceptive faculties.

The perennial psychology functions to gain a 'high ground' perspective. In common parlance, the 'high ground' is an elevated terrain that, in military terms, is considered useful in combat to gain the advantage. For use in the analogy here, the high ground can be said to offer an advantage in perception, allowing access to objective knowledge. By occupying the 'low ground' – so to speak

– a person's level of perception is not elevated. In this way, they are incapable of gaining an overarching view of events. Attention is focused onto the lesser, everyday matters and the issues-at-hand. This is the level of general cognition at which the majority of humankind exist.

The first requirement of any genuine initiatory stream is to release a person from their unconscious attachment to socio-cultural programming. Only in this way is a person capable of attaining to a 'clearer' perspective, free from the intervention of cultural filters. The next step would then entail a de-conditioning of a person's 'reality programming' that operates as the broader program above the cultural conditionings. As an example, cultural conditioning may involve religious beliefs and/or educationally-instilled information. Also, personal tastes in food, fashion, and entertainments, as well as emotional traits. Social conditioning, which is similar, may include specific ideologies, such as political, financial, and status systems. The 'reality programming' or conditioning includes the views we hold of our universe, our dimension, and material-paradigm. It is generally harder for a person to break-out of a reality paradigm as it is the larger structure that provides for us a sense of existence and a common perspective on life. Those experiences that disturb the reality programming (such as a near-death experience) usually affect us to a much greater degree than those that impact our social-cultural programming (such as travel or living abroad).

It will help if we remind ourselves that everything that we think we know is based on limited information. The usual way any of us gains knowledge is through the looking glass of our conditioned programs. Before going further, it is important to reflect upon this.

*****

Generally speaking, there are only two systems operating in the world. One is the systems 'of the world' such as political, social, scientific, cultural, etc. These systems have been created by people, for people, and rely heavily upon manipulations such as propaganda, conditioning, and consensus attitudes. The other system is 'not of the world' and can be best described as metaphysical. This system is much more complete and underlies everything within the known, visible reality. Most people, most of the time, are living and operating within the former system - the visible one. As such, reality as it is known adheres to the limited spectrum of the material and tangible. It is, however, the least part of Reality itself. This is not a criticism nor a judgement; it is stating a fact.

The British evolutionary biologist J.B.S. Haldane once said that 'the universe is not only queerer than we suppose, but queerer than we *can* suppose.' This can also be applied to the greater Reality. It is not only different from what we think it is – it is vastly different from anything we *can* think.

The perennial psychology is like a ground plan for humankind. It is an organized, structured body of knowledge that goes beyond any known form of formal teaching or education used within our cultural systems. It involves an extension of perception and advancement of cognition. The result is that it allows the person to comprehend the larger pattern of events within Reality. In our ordinary lives we are accustomed, and conditioned, to either subjectivity or relative objectivity. Genuine objectivity gives a person a new view vis-à-vis the cosmos and as such can be both unnerving and disconcerting to the unprepared person.

Whether it is fully understood or not, humankind is participating in a grand evolutionary journey that goes beyond our current conception of what evolution implies. The common understanding is of an incremental biological development over aeons, which is a patchy and incomplete picture at best. Simply put, any genuine wisdom teaching is of an evolutionary nature. To clarify, human beings are imprisoned within their limitations of perception and knowledge. As such, there are things unknown to us as well as many things we could be capable of doing. First, we must learn how to operate and function effectively within a constricted awareness of reality before this awareness can be expanded.

Another point to be noted is that many ancient systems of knowledge are no longer operative today despite their physical presence. That is, their once-active component has ceased to function correctly and as such they are not relevant according to their original purpose. It is not general knowledge that systems, including knowledge structures, are time and place specific. Just because a body of teaching was relevant for its time does not automatically mean it will still function or be relevant for today. Old ways, however valuable they once were, may not be suitable for the issues or contexts of contemporary times. All genuine teachings contain an essence - a blueprint – that can be extracted and modified to fit a new time and social context. Each stream of genuine wisdom is 'new' and fresh in its moment. It is necessary, for any source of knowledge, to be attentive to the features of the time and place in which it is operative.

It is said that regardless of what people think they do or do not do, it does not matter as what has to be done is done. It is done through us, and for us, and all we have to do is make ourselves available. The heart of the perennial psychology lives this truth – that we must make ourselves available and be ready to act upon unexpected opportunities. Humanity is being taken home. And there are *those people* operating within our midst who know how to take us home.

The perennial psychology functions as part of this work.

The perennial psychology places at our disposal tried and tested methods to actualize human capacity. To treat this as something 'magical' is to deny its true validity and to rob its potential. Genuine dynamic materials for human development are not the same as the ones used – and sold – in everyday life. It usually requires that a person first feels 'starved' until they are pushed to seek beyond the everyday materials. In this state of 'starvation,' a person is offered opportunities to also observe themselves. They may find they possess capacities which can be triggered by means other than social conditioning. In order to first be able to learn, a person must exercise capacities that are beyond everyday social patterning. This is sometimes referred to as *learning how to learn.*

The perennial psychology recognizes that the path to real development can begin when the following criteria are met: i) a recognition of one's situation and the need for self-development; ii) a partial detachment from one's social and cultural conditioning and external influences; and iii) beginning to work toward one's own liberty and inner freedom.

It is not possible to have immediate access to perennial Truth in any sustained way without first exhibiting a minimum of conscious awareness (as previously mentioned, glimpses may be possible). An individual works with relative truth until they are ready for higher Truth. That is, preparation by the use of relative truth. A phrase that is often used is – *the phenomenal is a bridge to the Real.*

The human being, like all of life, is involved in a continual process. An individual is usually only aware of a small part of this process. Life thus often seems to make no sense in the 'grand scheme' of things, as they say. To assist the new perceptual understanding to emerge, the old consciousness patterns must first be loosened by becoming less determined, dogmatic and fixed. Through this space, where old belief patterns and systems of thought are under scrutiny and found lacking, the advanced cognition enters. Part of the individual's effort is to do work on oneself to observe how the human personality is layered with artificial constructions, mental frameworks, and emotional triggers and safeguards. In other words, to methodically de-clutter the personality. The science of Self is very much a psychological intervention.

As human beings we need to guard against the disease of psychosclerosis – the hardening of attitudes that causes a person to cease dreaming, visioning, imagining, and learning. It is the hardening of the mind so that we become unteachable: we stop learning and we stop growing. In such states, a person can easily succumb to forms of social hypnotism and cultural brainwashing. Here is an old tale adopted to modern times:

There is a story which has existed in one form or another for as long as there have been human beings. The style of its telling changes with the time and place in which it is shared. In our day it begins with a very rich man who was the boss of a large company. As well as being rich he was also very mean, both in terms of his money as well as his behaviour toward others. He was so mean that he didn't want to hire supervisors to look after his employees, and instead expected his employees to get on with their jobs and to work all hours of every day. Of course, as is the way of people, the employees would often call in sick, take long breaks, and become distracted at work with chatting on social media with their friends. Eventually the boss became frustrated that his company was not performing as well as it should. Finally, the mean boss came up with a solution.

He found a magician who, for a little persuasion, was willing to hypnotize his employees. And so the boss had all of his employees hypnotized to believe that what they were doing was of great importance to the world and it gave them also much personal satisfaction. He also suggested to them that the meagre salary they were receiving was more than enough because they could apply for credit to buy all the things necessary for a comfortable life, such as a new television, a car, the latest phone and other gadgets, etc.

He also suggested to his employees that he was a good boss and that they should work hard for him, and not take any time off because any laziness would be an insult to the world that took care of them. To work hard to the very end of their lives, in fact, was a virtuous quality that made them 'good people.' And finally, for good measure, he decided to suggest to a few of his employees that they were better than the others, and deserved respect from their peers. And to some others he suggested that they needed to prove they were better than the others. In this way, he ensured that there would be enough personal rivalry and friction to keep his employees in competition amongst themselves.

And after that, as you can imagine, the mean boss had very few, if any, problems with his employees. But that didn't stop him from continuing to dislike them all!

It is said that a human being must develop by utilizing his or her own effort. To begin, an individual first needs to stabilize their consciousness. Each person has within them contact with an essential source, which at first may be a very narrow or slight contact, although precious. Development of that contact depends upon the efforts of each individual, and often requires a genuine guide to steer them. When correct, balanced, and harmonious development is cultivated, human cognition and comprehension may be transformed to another plane of perception. The Chinese alchemist Lu Tsu wrote in his poem:

'I must diligently plant my own field.
There is within it a spiritual germ that may live a thousand years.
Its flower is like yellow gold.
Its bud is not large, but its seeds are round
and like unto a spotless gem.

Its growth depends on the soil of the central palace,
but its irrigation must proceed from a higher fountain.
After nine years of cultivation,
root and branch may be transplanted
to the heaven of the higher genii.' [i]

The aim of inner development is also to transform material life. That is, for the external world to be transformed by a manifestation and expression of the new cognition and perception. The perennial path does not ask that a person steps back from the rigors and responsibilities of a material life to disappear into the subtle ethers, never to be heard from again. It is important that people are grounded in the world now, capable of absorbing fluctuations in perception whilst remaining socially active.

It may be the case that humanity has to reach a crisis point – in its materialism, commercialism, and social systems – for there to arise within people the need for something else. The human inner life now hungers and is reaching out for something more, something further. The need is for direct communion with something greater than which has been previously provided or offered by orthodox traditions. This developmental need to provide for a meaningful life - especially at a time of a deterioration in social and cultural systems - is not yet well-recognized among the highly industrialized, 'civilized' nations.

i Cited by William Alexander Parsons (1827-1916), in The Lore of Cathay, p. 59, 1901.

There should be no blame. Blame and name-calling serves no good purpose. Everyone, at some point, is at fault. Rumi said: 'If you are looking for a friend who is faultless, you will be friendless.' It will serve well to remember that those people who do not learn from the lessons of others will themselves become lessons for others.

The ability to handle life is also the ability to handle our own thoughts and emotions. To repeat, we are the looking glass through which we seek. It is not every person's duty to guide nations; yet it is our own duty to guide and rule our individual lives and our often-turbulent minds. Answers are eventually gained not through more words but by experience. Why talk about the taste of an apple when you know the taste?

It is not easy for a person to validate that which is unknown, and outside, the remit of their perceptions. We are trained and adapted to live in an environment of which we become accustomed. To break-out of this may not necessarily seem 'normal' to us, or even necessary. Yet when a person comes to realize that how they live and know their reality is a product of a limited perception, they may come to a different understanding.

Here is a tale to illustrate this:

'Once upon a time there was a city. It was very much like any other city, except it was almost permanently enveloped in storms.

The people who lived in it loved their city. They had, of course, adjusted to its climate. Living amid storms meant that they did not notice thunder, lightning and rain most of the time.

If anyone pointed out the climate they thought he was being rude or boring. After all, having storms was what life was like, wasn't it? Life went on like this for many centuries.

This would have been all very well, but for one thing: the people had not made a complete adaptation to a storm-climate. The result was that they were afraid, unsettled and frequently agitated.

Since they had never seen any other kind of place in living memory, cities or countries without some storms belonged to folklore and the babbling of lunatics.

There were two tried recipes which caused them to forget, for a time, their tensions: to make changes and to obsess themselves with what they had. At any given moment in their history, some sections of the population would have their attention fixed on change, and others on possessions of some kind. The unhappy ones would only then be those who were doing neither.

Rain poured down, but nobody did anything about it because it was not a recognized problem. Wetness was a problem, but nobody connected it with rain. Lightning started fires, which were a problem, but these were regarded as individual events without a consistent cause.

You may think it remarkable that so many people knew so little for so long.

But then we tend to forget that, compared to present day information, most people in history have known almost nothing about anything and even contemporary knowledge is daily being modified - and even proved wrong.'[1]

There are times when we need to submit to fate, and times when we may need to resist. Knowing this makes the difference.

References

[1] Shah, Idries. 1995. *The Magic Monastery*. London: The Octagon Press, p140.

Chapter Four

DE-CODING THE PATH

'The world has no being except as an appearance;
From end to end its state is a sport and a play.'
Shabistari

'The wind of God's grace is always blowing,
but you must raise your sail.'
Vivekananda

The term 'spiritualty' is nowadays more or less redundant of its essential value. It comes with too much cultural baggage and associated assumptions. It has also become highly commercialized, especially so since the late twentieth century. The use of it here is for a general understanding of advanced perceptions that lead to an expanded comprehension of Reality. Any language that is used is, of course, secondary to the phenomenon that is described or implied. Certain words will cease to have their popularity and will be replaced in time by others, as is often the case. Yet regarding matters of the spirit, they have been discussed, engaged with, and talked about since time immemorial. Such 'spiritual' concepts have been described as mysticism, esotericism, occult, metaphysical, and more.

Various teachings have operated throughout the centuries, including Hermeticism, Gnosticism, alchemy, Kabbalah, the magic/occult, as previously mentioned. They have also been operative through unknown or unsuspected cultural channels: 'Through these divine instruments the interior truths of the Sanctuary were taken into every nation, and modified symbolically according to their customs, capacity for instruction, climate, and receptiveness.' [1]

The perennial path has also operated through the Indian subcontinent in its Vedic literature (Rig Veda, the Brahmanas, the Aranyakas, and the Upanishads); as well as through some of the Greek schools (Platonism; Pythagaros; Neo-Platonism). It was notably active through Sufism during much of the Middle Ages (although the word 'Sufism' was coined by a German scholar only in the nineteenth century). More recently, it has been present within various paths of psychological development, under several names.

Matters concerning the development of perception have long been known as belonging to mysticism, generally because such comprehension is largely not accessible by the intellect. Mysticism, as well as some religious forms, have corresponded to a perception of the sacred. Religious structures were thus often used as historical vehicles and contexts within which to disseminate developmental impulses in accordance with their specific social-cultural norms. As has been noted, genuine wisdom is an active component separate from the forms, structures, and institutions through which it may choose to operate. A sincere developmental path is free from the dogmas that exist in all places and all times.

During times of religious and political tyranny the perennial psychology often continued its teaching in a more clandestine manner. In order to remain operative, it chose to work through the more orthodox and established institutions of the day, adhering to external protocols. Scholars or investigators of these known institutions often come across traces of these teachings and naively assume that the orthodox institution has a fixed 'mystical' side to it. They fail to recognize that the institution itself was being temporarily utilized as a carrier (like a shielding umbrella) for the transmission of a genuine wisdom stream. At times some well-known perennial teachers have been identified by mainstream researchers as representing these orthodox institutions and not, as is the case, working beyond appearances.

Appearances have been popular with lay-seekers. Westerners especially tend to over-orientalise teaching remnants and quickly associate them with a variety of commercial clichés - such as the robed guru, beads, incense, strange exotic diets, and oriental rituals such as whirling, and maybe even howling! These clichés exist because their physical remnants and traces still exist, yet they are but the leftovers from a once-active developmental operation. Often in the hands of unenlightened people they become the vehicle for cultish forms and commercial ventures that play upon people's need for attention.

These leftover remnants are obsolete and should not be confused with a genuine contemporary form of the perennial psychology. At best they are the displaced fragments of a once functional system of human development. As already stated, a genuine perennial path uses forms and methods appropriate to the time and culture in which it currently operates. Like a professional chef it uses ingredients 'locally sourced' and 'in season.' It does not import ingredients foreign to the palate of the local taster. Unfortunately, most of what is popularly recognized as being of the perennial path is a ragged collection of past fragments fused together and attractively packaged. As the phrase goes – *the dog may bark, but the caravan moves on.*

***

The essential self has no worldly desires. It is the social personality that collects and harbours such secondary desires. Within the realm of advanced perceptions there is no place for personal desires and satisfactions. These traces belong to a coarser mode of existence. Generally, religious and pseudo-spiritual paths have highlighted emotional conditioning. Greed has also been a dominant factor in some 'spiritual' paths, even when this is disguised as motivation. Often, the desire to want much in exchange for giving little is an unrecognized form of inner greed.

Providing emotional satisfaction is not the function of a genuine wisdom path. Emotional needs are first to be satisfied by social and cultural systems and institutions; they are not the remit of the developmental path. Deteriorated wisdom schools and religions function on this lesser domain of providing emotional and social support, often to the confusion of would-be seekers who are yet unable to verify a genuine source. Or, as is often the case, the persons are seeking superficial satisfactions despite their petitions to the contrary. It is a noticeable factor that many people who live balanced and fulfilled lives are not drawn to religious or similar institutions.

The role of emotion is not well understood in most western cultures. Emotional indulgence is often considered a desirable trait – even a healthy one. It is well understood that if a person eats too much, they will become overweight, leading eventually to obesity. Similarly, emotional indulgence can lead to obesity within a person's emotional centres. Many cultural impacts in the west are highly emotionally charged, and often deliberately so. Too much of this 'rich intake' can lead to emotional (and mental) imbalance, confusion, and disorientation. A brief glance at western societies will show that much emotional imbalance is already present. Such imbalance affects a person's ability to verify genuine impacts of a beneficial nature, such as those that trigger inner development. This is one of the reasons why pseudo-spiritual paths, 'guruism,' and spiritual exploitation and commercialization are so prevalent. When one lacks the means to credibly verify the role and function of a teaching, then one is vulnerable to manipulation and false agendas. This information is not new – it has been known for thousands of years. Today, however, we have the language and the psychological foundation upon which to better understand such concepts. Until one is equipped to calmly observe - and if need be to modify – one's behaviour, then one will continue to remain at the mercy of impacts and stimulations that may not be in one's best interests.

The same can be said for the role of the intellect. Its status is often unjustly exalted as such features as cleverness, cunning, and scholasticism are regarded as virtues in many of our societies. As a result, intellectualism and mental pursuits have become dominant tendencies, leading to excess and imbalance. Over-indulgence in emotional and intellectual stimuli can hamper access to objective knowledge. Here is a tale to consider:

'There was once a merchant who had a wife of great delicacy and of unsurpassed beauty. Unhappily, there came a time when the merchant ran into serious financial difficulties and was reduced to the verge of poverty. The reason for his difficulties was that many of his debtors had failed to pay him what they owed him.

Among his principal debtors was his greatest friend, a wealthy merchant, who had risen to his present state from being a greengrocer. He owed him 1000 gold pieces. The merchant was sure that his friend would help him in his time of adversity and need by repaying the debt. With this in mind, the approached his beautiful wife and asked her to visit his wealthy friend and to ask him for the repayment of the 1000 gold pieces. The wife agreed and soon set off to speak with the wealthy merchant. On being approached, the merchant graciously received the wife as his guest, but upon hearing her request for repayment he immediately began making excuses. He then said that he would repay the debt only if the beautiful wife would first satisfy his desires. This she refused to do, and immediately returned home to her husband to tell him everything that had happened.

The husband, on hearing his wife's story, was appalled, and told her to go to the local judge, who had originally been a calligrapher, and to plead for justice against the wealthy merchant, and so force him to repay his debt.

The local judge, on being approached, told the beautiful wife that he would certainly do what she asked, but only if she agreed to satisfy his desires. The wife refused and returned to tell her husband what had happened.

Stricken by the behaviour of the judge, the husband told his wife that she must go and ask the governor, who had previously been a soldier, to intervene and force the judge to behave properly.

Alas, the governor was no better than the other two, and said he would only oblige her if, first, she would oblige him. The wife refused and returned sorrowfully to report to her husband everything that had happened.

At that point, the wife did not know what to do, but while she was pondering the matter, a knock came at her door. When she answered it she found her one remaining servant, the night watchman. She and her husband had kept him because he was the one who remained awake when everyone else slept. The night watchman told her that he had learnt of what had happened and felt that he could help. He suggested that her problems could be solved by adopting a certain plan, but that the plan would have to be devious.

The plan was explained to the wife, who shortly afterwards sent a message to the wealthy merchant to say that if he would come to her apartments while her husband was away, she would be disposed to oblige him. The wealthy merchant came immediately, but just at the moment when he had stripped off all his clothes, there came a knock on the door by the night watchman. The wife showed every sign of alarm, saying it was her husband, and indicated that the merchant should jump into a box and hide. The wealthy merchant needed no second bidding and leapt quickly into the box. The wife then did the same thing with the judge and the governor, both of whom were locked away in separate boxes.

The beautiful wife then went to the King of the country, and explaining her predicament, asked him for his help, so that the three men should be punished, and the debt to her husband repaid. Having listened to this unlikely story, the King expressed disbelief and asked for proof. The wife immediately arranged for the three boxes to be brought before the King, and for them to be unlocked in his presence to reveal the three naked men. The King immediately perceived that the wife had told the truth, and immediately fined all three men. With the proceeds, he paid the poor merchant his dues, and then demoted the three offenders so that they were reduced once again to being a greengrocer, a calligrapher, and a soldier.'

According to tradition, this story represents all the aspects of a person's own psychological make-up. The poor merchant represents one's composite self. The wife can be regarded as one's essence – that part of oneself that is concerned with truth. The greengrocer represents the emotional part of oneself that is attached to things of the world. The calligrapher represents the intellect; and the soldier is the physical, organizing principle. The King represents outside intervention. Once the 'three men' (the three aspects of oneself) had been reduced to their original state, and the debt paid off, then everyone – as they say – lived happily ever after. Likewise, within a person, if the emotional, intellectual, and physical aspects are out of kilter, it is difficult for a person to 'prosper.' It is even more difficult for truth (the wife) to be dealt with fairly. It is all too easy for the emotional, intellectual, and physical aspects to grow 'too big for their boots' and to overpower the original harmony of a person's being. In this state, correct and balanced learning upon an inner path is almost impossible. It is the function of perennial psychology to address these issues within any potential learner. Hence, the need for dealing with a person's social conditioning as well as with the balance of their emotional, intellectual, and physical states.

The way of the perennial psychology is a subtle path that seemingly provides little in the form of tangible - or ritualistic - guidelines. It does not excite or promote itself. Strange or eccentric behaviour is not required. A genuine path of knowledge is the very essence of normality within the culture it is operative.

It is said that human beings have three possible modes of operation. The first is the normal mode of conditioned life. It is produced from a mix of culture and environment, as well as the specific moral and value systems. Included here are such belief systems as religion and political-social ideologies. Such dominant ideologies as rationalism, industrialism, and capitalism have represented these conditioned value systems in recent years. The truth of the situation is that although a person will believe that they are behaving, and thinking, according to what they feel are their deepest beliefs and personal convictions, they are in fact only acting out their particular cultural programming. In this mode of life, a person is not able to perceive that they do not know who they are nor what their purpose is.

Instead of attempting to deal with this blindness people will seek to distract themselves through pursuing what they believe to be meaningful goals, not realizing they are actually pointless. Examples can be found throughout social, cultural, and educational systems, events, and entertainments.

The next mode of operation is through a reactional response to cultural norms. That is, by actively seeking an expression of rebellion. Such expressions are believed by people to be morally significant, and of merit. People may believe they are 'making a stand' whereas they may only be reinforcing another position of conditioning. People may also be strengthening their false personality and its ego. Such examples can be seen in 'alternative' lifestyles and in fashion extremes and sub-culture identifications. A recent historical expression was manifested in the various revolutionary acts during the 1960s – including the 'flower-power' hippie generation as well as the student protests.

The third mode of human operation lies in objective perception which brings with it real knowledge. This mode of existence is operating all the time, unbeknown to the majority of humankind. It can be said that we are the fish in the sea seeking the illusive mystery of water. This mode is seldom perceived because of the reliance upon the previous two modes of cultural conditioning. To increase perception of this mode requires that a person observes, recognizes, and acts upon deep levels of social programming. To not grasp, or admit to, such deep programming is an instant blockage upon the way to deeper realization. The dilemma facing a person here is that this finer mode of operation cannot be verified by ordinary means, or by those filters provided by social and cultural systems. The game-rules that program our social lives do not permit the realization of these finer modes of perception. They are literally not a part of the everyday game. Yet within ordinary life it is possible to gain verification of this mode through receiving information that cannot be obtained in any other way. Some of these 'interventions' have been historically classed as 'miracles.' What we may take to be *distortions* in reality ('anomalies') may in fact be an indication of a greater Reality in operation within the lesser mode of ordinary life.

In general, human societies operate through a lack of knowledge and awareness. This is evident by what is witnessed in terms of aggression, insecurity, warfare, immorality, and general infantile acts of competitive behaviour at the global level. Politics firmly functions within the first mode of operation. The first step that any person can take is to become aware of automatic pattern-thinking, and to observe the socio-cultural indoctrinated values that limit human perception and receptivity. In this regard, the following three stages can be considered:

i) AWARENESS – of our predicament & perspective

ii) PREPARATION – for stepping onto the path

iii) PERCEPTION – the gaining of objective understanding

The first stage - Awareness - requires self-examination and observation upon social-cultural conditioning and the way the 'false self' behaves. The second stage – Preparation – is about developing the capacity to receive finer impacts as distinct from cruder ones. This involves stepping back from the distracting acquisitions of everyday life – our opinions, useless thoughts, acquired attitudes, etc. The third stage – Perception - is received according to the capacity of the individual. It is known as Truth – there is no room for belief, or other secondary features. Of this, nothing more can be said.

The realm of higher perception is capable of verification, as in all experience and realization. Each person can have a so-called 'spiritual experience,' yet they need to acquire the capacity to follow it and verify it for themselves. People often take their own absence of experience as proof of its absence or absurdity. It is well to remember that people incapable of judgments on such matters should refrain from making them.

Truth has no fixed form. However, to perceive the Greater Truth we are compelled to work through fixed forms, including our corporeal selves. All such forms are limited in that they are relative to time, place, and variable contexts. All forms belong to a transitory, external world. As such, they do not have permanency. Human civilization is filled with forms in varying states of existence and decay. People have invariably been attracted to decaying forms, unaware that their essential usefulness is no longer operative. Attraction to form over substance will blind a person to receiving what otherwise could be beneficial to their inner growth. Forms are vehicles for transmission and should be viewed as such. In this regard, like all packaging, they will outlive their usefulness at some point – unless modified and readapted.

To repeat, the perennial psychology has operated throughout the ages and through various forms, with varying names, and with multiple appearances. The essence of a genuine source of knowledge remains unequivocal, regardless of its manner of expression. As it is often said: 'Things that are in opposition outwardly, may be working together inwardly.'

The perennial path recognizes that there is a purposeful correspondence between patterns and processes in the cosmos and events and happenings (impacts) here upon the terrestrial plane. Above all, the path recognizes balance and harmony between that which is transcendent and that which is terrestrial – between the 'above' and the 'below;' between the 'inner' and the 'outer.' Where there is no harmony – no grace – there is no true correspondence.

Humanity's greatness is not in what it has achieved, nor what it is, but in what it can become. The reader would do well to remember that the path of inner transformation is not a straight path. Nor is it what it may be imagined to be.

References

[1] Eckhartshausen, Karl von. *The Cloud Upon the Sanctuary*. 2016. Cadiz: Azafran Books.

Chapter Five

IN THE MIND'S EYE

'Your medicine is in you, and you do not observe it.
Your ailment is from yourself, and you do not register it.'
Hazrat Ali

'Make mankind your dwelling place.'
Hariri

The purpose of any perennial psychology activity is to further the objective of its work alongside human development. People who are essentially interested in themselves over and above the ongoing Work will not progress beyond the early stages. Work that initially begins on oneself will inevitably, if it is in alignment, come to represent work for others and for the Path. This is the threefold nature of the perennial psychology. It is work for oneself, for others, and for the larger context of the Path. In this way, it is said that the perennial psychology has an evolutionary function.

It is necessary that a person approaching such a path of knowledge possesses a minimum of awareness about themselves. Self-observation is a least requirement, not an achievement. That is why a path of knowledge is both an inner science as well as a psychological body of teaching. A particular feature of the modern world today is that psychological knowledge and understanding is known and widespread. This knowledge base provides a language for technical terms which were previously transmitted through 'folk wisdom.' Concepts such as obsession, belief systems, conditioning, delusion, false self, etc., were historically maintained through common traditions such as tales, stories, legends, and jokes. For example, many people can recognize an Aesop fable - such as the race between the hare and the tortoise - yet few people understand how these tales operate through a specific function.

Similarly, today we have current knowledge upon how the left and right brain hemispheres function. A modern psychological and neurological language exists to explain how the left/right hemispheres process information and knowledge. Previously, this was not common understanding; yet certain tales and jokes were utilized to trigger and strengthen the hemispheric brain functioning. It was not talked about, yet the underlying knowledge was applied by *those who knew*. This is but one brief example of how the perennial psychology has been operating through human cultures.

The modes, practices, and processes of mystical (esoteric) activities are now beginning to be more understood.

This includes techniques for training intuition - such as the practices of meditation, body postures and movements, martial arts, mantras, visualization exercises, deep prayer, and so on. They all share a common physiological basis – they act to stimulate the right hemisphere of the human brain. A correct and functioning correspondence between these two hemispheres constitutes an 'organ of perception' that is present in everyone yet under-developed in most people. Certain practices and exercises, for example, can trigger specific states of consciousness that then affect biological structures. In general terms, a human mind that functions more through left/right hemispheric integration can process a heightened form of perception. It is for this reason that many ancient teachings include stories, tales, allegories, that serve to stimulate, and activate, left/right brain functioning, from which a more integral consciousness (i.e., advanced cognition) can emerge.

The normal, 'everyday' perception that people process depicts a linear, horizontal relationship with the external world. This has served to cut off humanity from a more participatory and expansive relationship with the cosmic environment. The perennial psychology operates within a reality of more profound depth and scale. The perennial path is both a cultural phenomenon as well as a distinct psychological science.

Psychological activity as it is generally applied is for the crude conditioned 'secondary self' and not for the essential self. This applied psychology operates within the social domain, often with issues relating to the false personality. Contact with a genuine source of perennial psychology aims first to stabilize this secondary self and to integrate it into society. It is important at this stage not to confuse emotional responses with 'higher experiences' which can often be the case. This phenomenon has been central to the rise of cults over the years. An unbalanced response to what people believe to be their own 'higher experiences' has also fuelled the therapeutic industry in recent years. It is important that a person deals with therapy issues, or the need for cult participation, before approaching a genuine source of teaching. Any true body of knowledge operates through a highly developed science of human psychology. No matter what we may think, we can neither fool 'it' nor our own true selves.

The emphasis that the perennial path has on inner development makes it compatible with modern forms of psychotherapy. According to leading psychologist Robert E. Ornstein, in his textbook, *The Psychology of Consciousness*:

> 'A new synthesis is in process within modern psychology. This synthesis combines the concerns of the esoteric traditions with the research methods

> and technology of modern science. In complement to this process, and feeding it, a truly contemporary approach to the problems of consciousness is arising from the esoteric traditions themselves.'[1]

Both the perennial path and modern psychology deal with similar issues, including the fundamental human need for meaning. Many modern socio-cultural institutions are no longer able to account or provide for meaning. This lack of meaning in modern life can both stimulate a person to seek out a path of inner development, as well as triggering states of despair or ennui.

A feeling of hopelessness and despair can result from a distortion of reality. In the extreme, these states can transform into unhealthy fantasies and delusions. The same is true for society as it is for the individual. That is, an entire culture - even an entire civilization - can be at the mercy of its own distorted view of reality and its associated delusions. The perennial psychology claims that humankind is psychologically 'ill' because people are generally unable to perceive who they really are and what their situation is. That is why, in technical terms, they are referred to as being 'blind' or 'asleep' because their higher capacity remains dormant and underdeveloped. Life for the average person is about manifesting lesser capacities; such as greed, desire, need for attention and emotional stimulation.

In perennial mystical traditions the development of the necessary perception is often called 'awakening,' and the perception itself is called 'knowledge.' The science of awakening is the aim of perennial psychology and, it is said, it has been with humankind for thousands of years, in one form or another. The perennial psychology has never been wholly absent from human life, although it has not always been so readily available. It is a path that must be sought. It does not seek the seeker. Nor can it be so easily offered to each person alike.

The knowledge is taught according to the needs of each particular culture in which it operates. The form of its presentation/transmission is what can be called a 'cultural carrier' – not to be confused with the content. The Persian sage Rumi famously said – *Do not look at my outward shape, but take what is in my hand.* As one recent teacher put it - we do not study the life of animals by the dead skin they have left behind, so why do it for the study of a living knowledge? In our normal mode of thinking we do not recognize that the human range of perception is so limited. Or that the regular level of experience excludes a significant dimension of reality. For this reason, the perennial path teaches that the purpose of human life lies beyond the perceptual range of the ordinary person. To widen that range is the aim of a genuine teaching. Hence, one of the first steps is to recognize, and accept, that ideas and views about the world are only descriptions of the world. It is necessary that latent faculties of perception are stimulated. Here is a revealing anecdote:

> 'I was once in a certain country where the local people had never heard the sounds emitted from a radio receiver. A transistorized set was being brought to me; and while waiting for it to arrive I tried to describe it to them. The general effect was that the description fascinated some and infuriated others. A minority became irrationally hostile about radios. When I finally demonstrated the set, the people could not tell the difference between the voice from the loudspeaker and someone nearby. Finally, like us, they managed to develop the necessary discrimination of ear, such as we have. And, when I questioned them afterwards, all swore that what they had imagined from descriptions of radios, however painstaking, did not correspond with the reality.'[2]

The perennial psychology views ordinary life as being like a trance state. Within this state of restricted awareness and conditioned behaviour a person functions within a framework of socio-cultural roles, and basic cognition. In technical terms, it is referred to as a *lesser reality*. This lesser reality is filled with fantasies, illusions, and delusions. Such a life of partial awareness may be referred to as a state of 'adequate dysfunction.' It is adequate in that a person can make most ordinary tasks necessary for a regular life whilst in this state. At the same time, however, a person does not suspect that the state is incomplete, and thus partly dysfunctional. The human condition is veiled to the ordinary person. Any unsolicited instances of momentary awakening are generally regarded as anomalies.

Contrary to what people may believe, it is our own individual responsibility to develop the capacity for higher perception. It is similar to a person living a whole life overseas in a foreign environment without bothering to learn any of the local language. In this state, the ordinary person remains 'asleep' because of the reliance upon conditioned thought patterns and limited perceptions. Any experience of reality is therefore likewise constricted.

The perennial psychology claims that the development of latent perceptual capacities is not only vital for well-being and happiness, but that it is the principle aim of the current phase of existence. In other words, it is a part of the present evolutionary endeavour. As in Rumi's opening quote in Chapter One, if we do everything else in this life but that 'one thing' then we shall have done nothing.

As stated, psychological knowledge and understanding is known and widespread in the world today. A perennial path corresponds to aspects of modern psychotherapy as both work towards changing automated patterns of thinking and perception. These issues often underlie many of modern society's ills. The perennial psychology has worked with these human imbalances for millennia, often unknown to orthodox, mainstream practices.

Perennial traditions have a deep and sophisticated understanding of perception and its relation to cognition and the human psyche. It is not a therapeutic system, although the diminishing or eradication of mental/ emotional imbalance are by-products of inner development. Like any good science, the wisdom traditions require special training and knowledge in order to gain credible results. Nothing upon the perennial path is haphazard - except for the human personality!

Modern science tends to largely ignore the fact that correct awareness and perception is fundamental to human life. Self-awareness and balanced self-observation are the basis for conscious inner development. Without a minimal degree of self-awareness, a person is unable to step outside of conditioned thoughts and beliefs. A primary tenet of the perennial path is that reality, as ordinarily perceived by the average person, is a distortion. Also, that much human suffering and emotional anguish comes as a result of believing in and supporting this distorted view. Perennial wisdom traditions have existed in order to provide means for the human being to perceive the meaning of life and the larger purpose of existence. True meaning is fundamentally a question of perception. According to the perennial tradition, the knowledge that comes from heightened perception allows a person to know the meaning of human life, both in terms of the micro (the events of a person's life) and the macro (the destiny of the human race). In short, the development of the higher, perceptual capacity that is inherent in human beings is vital to their happiness. This fact is seldom recognized.

The recent phase in human civilization, in the west particularly, has developed cultures that are psychologically orientated. Because of this, genuine manifestations of the perennial traditions that are operative in the western hemisphere use the form and appearance of psychological teachings. Genuine wisdom traditions have always sought to develop conscious awareness and perceptual capacities within the human individual. It is only that they often formed part of the religious and spiritual streams within human civilization and hence made use of their appropriate vocabulary and technical terminology. However, the principal aim is for the individual to gain the capacity to perceive the reality that underlies the phenomenal world of ordinary experience.

To reiterate, these modern forms of the perennial wisdom path use the terminology that most people are 'asleep.' This refers to a person's everyday consciousness being occupied – or programmed – by automated thought patterns, beliefs, and ideas. These are constructs that, layer upon layer, come to create a human personality. Each personality is conditioned according to the social and cultural norms, customs, and regulations of the immediate environment (including the governing authority). These cultural programs help in cultivating regional and national identities that are then socially manageable in order to maintain, and stabilize, large human communities (such as nation states). Throughout a person's life they are impacted, and thus influenced, by a large range of social-cultural conditioning that follows them until physical death. These external impacts (programming) block the mind to receiving finer degrees of perception. That is, they serve to occupy the mind as a form of 'mental hijack.' It is the function of the perennial teaching to 'unblock' these impacts and obstacles in order to free the mind toward higher development and cognition. Only then is a person able to perceive the true significance of human life in both the micro and macro levels. A generalized, and basic form, of this perception in people is what is referred to as intuition.

Intuition is the faculty of knowing without the use of rational processes. It is sometimes called indirect knowing, or direct cognition. This form of knowing – a direct knowledge of Reality – is what the perennial teaching aims to cultivate. The faculties of reason, on the other hand, are the lower, human-centric processes.

The perennial path constitutes an integral system that requires the correct cultural context in which to operate. As previously stated, this constitutes appropriate timing, a suitable culture, and the right people. Together these elements constitute a functional, integral system that operates as a whole. To break them into their parts would be to destroy the functionality of the whole. This is similar to the boy who dismembered the fly and then wondered where the fly had gone to.

The perennial tradition also takes into account whether a particular culture is ready or prepared for a particular transmission. It may be that a culture is ripe for a transmission (seeding) and the activation (harvesting) will come at a later time or several generations in the future. Since the perennial psychology is a developmental science, and not a dogma or a rigid technique, it must respond to and operate within the broader social and cultural environment. It does not exist in isolation. As the opening quote to this chapter indicates - *'Make mankind your dwelling place.'* (Hariri).

Over the years people, including various 'seekers-of-truth,' have complained that wisdom paths are either hard to find or are deliberately ambiguous, or evasive. It is worth noting that it is the commercial, and often superficial, schools that are easy to find and easily accessible. The genuine perennial wisdom traditions do not go after students. They neither missionize nor advertise. In many cases, they are not publicly known, and some may indeed not be operating as teaching paths. What most systems fail to account for is that the perennial path is only for those who already lead balanced and stable social lives. To repeat, the wisdom path is not a therapy. Those who are able to obtain satisfaction from daily life and worldly affairs are not looking for compensation from a developmental path. That is, such people can satisfy their need for attention from ordinary life. Once this 'attention energy' has been satisfied, a person is more suitable to approach a path of learning. The perennial psychology does not exist for the entertainment of individuals – that can be left to the colourful gurus of the world to satisfy. Their presence serves a useful function in that it filters out those people seeking 'easy enlightenment' from those with capacity to see beyond.

The need to be balanced and socially stable is often underestimated, or in its extreme it is ignored altogether. It is worth noting that greed makes a person believe things they would not normally believe. The same applies for greed in 'spiritual' matters. A change in a person's state of consciousness can be misinterpreted, misleading, or even dangerous, if a person is not suitably prepared. The most basic of results for an unprepared person are that it may increase their egocentricity and sense of superiority. In other cases, it may result in paranoia. Self-delusion, fantasies of grandeur, and magical thinking are also features that manifest within the unprepared person. History is littered with such cases, even when such traits are lauded by the society in which they operate.

The would-be student must take care not to waste energies on pursuing the exotic, the delightful, the easily accessible, and the most glamorous promotions. A glossy webpage is least likely to lead to a permanent state of heightened perception. A genuine perennial teaching will not appear dressed in the garb of a foreign culture. It will exist on your doorstep – and in a form least expected. It will appear normal. It may even appear 'boring.' The perennial wisdom traditions operate through the cultural channels open to them in accordance with their location and social norms. At the present time, this is likely to include western psychological understanding. It is within this context that any potential student is afforded the means to ready themselves.

References

[1] Ornstein, R. E. 1972. *The Psychology of Consciousness*. San Francisco: W. H. Freeman & Co., p. 244

[2] Shah, Idries. 1995. *The Magic Monastery*. London: The Octagon Press, p116

Chapter Six

READYING THE SELF

'Higher knowledge, higher meaning, if it falls on the ordinary level of understanding, will either seem nonsense, or it will be wrongly understood...'

Aldous Huxley

'What is brought to you depends on the reception you give to it.'

Rudolph Steiner

'Knowledge gives nothing to a man until he gives everything to it.'

Ancient proverb

It can be said that, within the grander scheme, a person lives for a relatively short span of time. The things which happen to a person often offer far more potential than the things a person causes to happen. In order to be more effective, a person is called upon to dominate their inner environment. By developing inner faculties, an individual has the capacity to 'act' with intention. Intention is a form of deliberate creation. Such an individual then can live as a guiding force for others. Yet the way of the perennial tradition is not an easy one for the very reason that it is subtle. The contemporary person, especially in western cultures, is accustomed to receiving what may be termed as more brutal impacts. The patience and understanding required for a genuine perennial teaching path lay beyond the impacts of modern stimuli. The developmental path is not the quick fix. Neither is it replete with readily identifiable results. It belongs to the individual who feels or senses a *different type* of need within them. For want of a better word, it can be referred to as a 'calling.' The perennial tradition has always existed in order to respond to a particular calling within humanity.

People can be quick to declare their interest in such a path, yet in many cases they lack essential motivation. It is a recognized feature of human psychology that things which glitter attracts the false personality. As the well-known phrase goes – 'all that glitters is not gold.' Contemporary society is full of sparkling attractions that whilst they may entertain, they also serve to distract. What a person wants is often not the same as what they need. Many wants are based on inventions, fantasies, or even delusions. An individual's desires are a labyrinth that requires careful navigation. Also, each person usually has a preconceived idea of *how* they want to receive something; not knowing that the transmission of knowledge cannot be dictated. When an impact, experience or a learning, arrives contrary to expectations it is likely to be ignored or even rejected. Human assumptions have stood in the way of the developmental path since the beginning.

As the previous chapter indicated, the path to a first beginning is strewn with conditioned thinking. The first step that is required, therefore, is for a person to become aware of their conditioned patterns of thinking. It is a common trait that most people, regardless of status, start out with an ingrained, conditioned vanity towards inner development. This is expressed in the following tale:

There is an eastern story about a sage who asked his disciples to recount what their vanities had been before they had come to study with him.
The first said – 'I imagined myself to be a beautiful person who was admired by many.'
The second said – 'I believed myself to be superior to others because I was seeking a greater truth.'
The third said – 'I believed I had the capacity to become a teacher.'
And the fourth said – 'My vanity was greater than all these, for I believed that I could learn!'
The sage replied – 'And the fourth disciple's vanity remains the greatest, for his vanity is to show that he once had the greatest vanity.'

The path of the perennial tradition requires that an individual first must be capable of detaching from conditioned programming, including assumptions, opinions, and biased judgements. A person must also be aware of their social and emotional needs, which previously exerted an influence upon them and the choices they made. The developmental path is aligned with that of conscious evolution. It can be said that the past ten thousand years of human history has provided for the possibility for conscious evolution. In other words, the human species has been afforded the possibility to develop through deliberate and directed effort, rather than through random impacts. This understanding, and what is signifies, is crucial for the future.

The path forward begins first with oneself. There is no other way. The human individual is the beginning and end of the journey – the alpha and the omega. To arrive at the Source is the same as to arrive at Oneself.

Jewish philosophy recognizes the notion of *teshuvah,* which implies a returning inwardly to the divine Source. This inward turning is a part of daily practice to retain the connection, and which assists personal transformation upon psychological and social levels. This inward returning is an aspect of the perennial path. It is constant movement. It does not stop for lunch time, or when we go to sleep. This is the subtle connection that corresponds with the *eternal movement* of the seeker-of-truth.

People who believe themselves in need of a 'spiritual' path may instead be seeking some form of relief from tension, stress, or similar issues in daily life. The caveat here is that by embarking upon a developmental path, it may instead cause personal issues to be amplified rather than diminished. As already noted, it is an unhealthy mistake, although a common one, to mix inner development with therapy. It is important not to confuse these two distinct needs.

The first step in preparing for a developmental path is honesty with oneself. The journey cannot truly begin without one's honesty and sincerity. As one commentator put it – 'Responsibility, sincerity, humility, patience, and generosity - these are not ends in themselves but are tools that must be acquired before a person can proceed further.'[1] These core values, as well as ordinary forms of knowledge – gained through observation and reasoning – are necessary for our lives. However, their presence does not deny that a higher knowledge is also available; and awaits those who are prepared to work to receive it. Ordinary states of consciousness are considered the norm because they are the dominant experience. Yet this does not invalidate other states of consciousness and perception. The initial steps toward this more rarefied experience begin within ordinary life. The following quote recognizes this, and is given in length:

> 'Esoteric knowledge can be given only to those who seek, only to those who have been seeking it with a certain amount of consciousness, that is, with an understanding of how it differs from ordinary

> knowledge and how it can be found... This preliminary knowledge can be gained by ordinary means, from existing and known literature, easily accessible to all. And the acquisition of this preliminary knowledge may be regarded as the first test. Only those who pass this first test, those, that is, who acquire the necessary knowledge from the material accessible to all, may hope to take the next step, at which point direct individual help will be accorded them. A man may hope to approach esotericism if he has acquired a right understanding from ordinary knowledge, that is, if he can find his way through the labyrinth of contradictory systems, theories and hypotheses, and understanding their general meaning and general significance. This test is something like a competitive examination open to the whole human race, and the idea of a competitive examination alone explains why the esoteric circle appears reluctant to help humanity. It is not reluctant. All that is possible is done to help men, but men will not or cannot make the necessary efforts themselves. And they cannot be helped by force.'[2]

The perennial psychology recognizes that there needs to be a corresponding level of development within the person for them to be able to receive the initial transmission of knowledge. In contemporary cultures especially, a person may be deemed as clever (they may know a great deal) yet their understanding is lacking because of their state of being. That is why it is often said in perennial literature that 'the secret protects itself.'

Perennial wisdom is a highly developed science (an inner technology) that reveals its meaning in accordance to the capacity of the person who approaches it. Such a path, and its adherents, attempts neither to missionize nor convince people of either its presence or its truth. It does not need to. Often it is the contrary, in that the responsibility lies with the person to convince those of the perennial path of their sincerity. Despite what people may think (which is usually based on faulty, conditioned patterns), access to the perennial wisdom is not an automatic right but a privilege to be earned by correct efforts. As Rudolf Steiner alludes to in the opening quote to this chapter, the type of knowledge that comes to a person depends on that person's ability, or capacity, *to receive* it.

As mentioned at the outset, people are often quick to declare their interest yet soon lose it when confronted by alternatives which may be more attractive or externally convincing. Here is a well-known ancient tale given in contemporary form:

> *There was once a well-known television stage magician and hypnotist who amassed a great wealth from his regular appearances in the media. Soon he decided to build for himself a large house near a well-to-do and prosperous village. When the house was finished, he invited all the people of the village to dinner. The locals were all very excited and were much looking forward to meeting their famous host. They all arrived in their best clothes and jewellery hanging from their arms.*

The famous television host appeared and said - 'Before we eat, we have some entertainments.'

Everyone was thrilled and pleased, and the magician host provided a first-class conjuring show, with rabbits coming out of hats, flags appearing from nowhere, and one thing turning into another. The people were delighted. Then their host asked: 'Would you like dinner now, or more entertainments?'

Everyone called for more entertainments, for they had never seen anything like it before; at home there was food, but never such excitement as this. So the famous hypnotist changed himself into a pigeon, then into a hawk, and finally into a phoenix that rose from the ashes. The people went wild with excitement.

He asked them again, and they wanted more. And so, they got more entertainment. Finally, he asked them if they wanted to eat, and they said that they did. So, their hypnotist host made them feel that they were eating, diverting their attention with a number of tricks, through his deceptive powers.

The imaginary eating and entertainments went on all night. When it was dawn, some of the people said, 'We must go to work.' So, the host made those people imagine that they went home, got ready for work, and actually did a day's work.
In short, whenever anyone said that they had to do something, the host made them think first that they were going to do it, then, that they had done it and finally that they had come back to the stage magician's house.

Finally, the host had woven such spells over the people of the village that they worked only for him while they thought that they were carrying on with their ordinary lives. Whenever they felt a little restless, he made them think that they were back at dinner at his house, and this gave them pleasure and made them forget.

And what happened to the magician and the people, in the end? Do you know, I cannot tell you, because he is still busily doing it, and the people are still largely under his spell.

The perennial path is a body of knowledge – or body of technique - that has existed for the purpose of stimulating people into higher levels of perception and cognition. The first stage occurs through the activation of preparatory states. Initiatory stimuli that act on a person's psychic being may include books and stories that, because of their construction, allow for cultural longevity. Into this transmission also falls many fairy tales, fables, myths, and parables. Without it being known, human cultures are in fact participating with what may loosely be called the metaphysical realm. That is, the realm of higher knowledge is constantly meshing with the ordinary world. If this was not the case, it is likely that human civilization would have perished before now. This confluence of the higher and lower worlds is part of the matrix that sustains life within current modes of reality. Access to these perceptive realms has often been activated through the power of creative imagination.

Within perennial literature there has always been a distinction between what is 'true imagination' and what is fantastical imagination. In the ordinary sense, the power of the imagination has been degraded to things of fantasy, wishful thinking, and the like. It is said that someone has an active imagination if they are something of a dreamer. It is used as both a positive as well as derogative term. We may tell our children to stop daydreaming. Or a friend may say 'get real' or 'get in the real world' if they feel you are using too much of the imagination. Yet the occult use of the imagination is much more focused, specific, and is itself a science. With a trained use of the imagination comes techniques of visualization, concentrated will, and projection of psychic force. Imagination used with intention is a fundamental energy known as deliberate creation. There are sources where the reader can turn to if they wish to learn more about the history and uses of active imagination. Here, I make only a suggestive reference for the attentive reader.

The process of 'true imagination' can activate certain psychic energies within a person, which then stimulates a heightened range of perceptions not generally offered in ordinary life. The stimulation of true imagination has a transformative power that acts on the external world and shifts how the world is viewed. In one context, there is a correspondence to what has been known as the 'imaginal world.' Aspects of this can be found in the lineage of Persian theosophy, oriental Gnosticism, Neo-Platonism, Cabbalism, Hermeticism, Sufic material, Romantic poetry, and more. More recently, this theme has been intellectually explored in the research work of Henry Corbin. The 'imaginal world' both exists beyond the everyday, mundane reality, as well as participating with it. This may sound contradictory, yet it makes sense when understood. The everyday, fantastical imagination is often regarded as the lower, wasteful use of the human being's imaginative faculty. What often begins in dreams may end up as part of known reality. That is why it is said that 'in dreams begin responsibilities.' The Neo-Platonic philosopher Plotinus said that we perceive things in correspondence with our soul. The beauty we perceive, he said, is a reflection of the soul's state. Similarly, the Romantic poet William Blake wrote the line - 'The Suns Light when he unfolds it/*Depends on the Organ that beholds it.*' More recently, the famous physicist Albert Einstein was asked in an interview whether he trusted his imagination more than his knowledge. He replied – 'Imagination is more important than knowledge. Knowledge is limited. Imagination encircles the world.'

The forms of collective imagination expressed in any given epoch influences the manifestation and unfolding of events in the external world. On the whole, however, the average person is unaware of how the external 'objectified' world responds to the inner psyche of the human being. Advanced perception understands that the dominant view of life is sterile. The perennial path requires that a person frees themselves from this 'sleeping' relation to phenomena, and enters into a live, waking relationship. Perennial psychology teaches that what we take to be the external world is not independent of us. Furthermore, that base reality is inseparable from the inner world of human thought. The inner state of the human being has a role to play in determining what type of future world will emerge. It is that real – both a frightening yet also a wondrous possibility. For this reason, careful steps are required.

In the perennial tradition, knowledge cannot be withheld from a person who is qualified to receive it. Likewise, it cannot be given to a person unprepared for its reception. The ability to receive knowledge is a functional matter and is not a question of personal opinion or emotional judgement. Upon a genuine path, a person does not *earn* knowledge as a form of reward. Rather, they work to make themselves capable of receiving it. An ancient proverb says: 'Nobody and nothing can stand between you and knowledge if you are fit for it; but anybody and anything can stand between you and knowledge if you are not fit for it.' There are no shortcuts upon the way, no matter how much people demand it. A cleansing process must first take place as part of the preparation. This is a beginning and not an end goal, as many may think. The process of deconditioning is at the early stage of the path and is not the end result. It can take years for a person to detach from mental and emotional conditioned patterns. Yet it is a fundamental necessity. A person is simply unable to perceive a greater understanding of Reality if they are attached to a lesser reality that is constructed from an artificial mix of beliefs, opinions, and cultural myths. No matter how deeply interested a person is in a developmental path, they are required to receive a minimum level of genuine experiences. Intellectual understanding is no substitute for actual experience. In the words of one commentator:

> 'Words alone do not communicate; there must be something prepared, of which the words are a hint. Practice alone does not perfect humanity. Man needs the contact of the truth, initially in a form which will help him.' (Nazir el Kazwini)

The perennial psychology operates through a correspondence between the creative 'true imagination' and a disciplined mental concentration. The preparation concerns developing the capacity to receive knowledge. This sometimes corresponds to what is recognized as receiving inspiration. The perennial path serves to both develop the individual internally as well as developing socio-cultural conditions externally. As mentioned, perennial wisdom works through human communities as an integral presence; it operates in part as a civilizing impulse upon the planet. The true path is one of service, beyond the self, toward fellow humanity, and for the greater Truth.

Humanity reflects a psychological state that is under continual development. Under the correct conditions a person may be 'awakened' to perceiving this process and allowed to participate in its advancement. A genuine tradition understands that once a person has perceived the greater Reality, then they are to proceed on their own. A defining aspect of the perennial tradition is that the function of the teacher is to make themselves redundant. That is, their role is to work themselves out of a job. The aspirant, having achieved their goal, then works through their own connection and contact.

The direct intuition of the greater reality signifies an evolutionary stage of human evolution and which is the destiny of the human race. Any aspiring seeker is expected to ready themselves for understanding these vital truths and to know how to apply it to their time. This is part of the genuine evolutionary work. As it is said:

'Seek wisdom while you have the strength, or you may lose strength without gaining wisdom.'

References

[1] Deikman, Arthur. *'Sufism and Psychiatry'* in Shah, Idries, ed. 1979. The World of the Sufi. London: Octagon Press, p195

[2] Ouspensky, PD. 1969. *A New Model of the Universe.* New York: Knopf.

Chapter Seven

WISE CRACKS

'An elephant and a mouse who were in love decided to get married. On their wedding night, the elephant keeled over and died. The mouse said: "Oh Fate! I have bartered one moment of pleasure for a lifetime of digging a grave!"' [i]

'Someone engaged in self-study should not have a fool for a teacher'
Proverb

The perennial psychology can be very funny. It can make you laugh out loud. Participating as part of an evolutionary process is not all serious faces and sternness. On the contrary, a good sense of humour is definitely required. All applicants for the post must know at least one good joke. If you don't have a sense of humour, please don't apply. Go and find yourself some good dogma to chew on.

There was once a man who joined a distance-learning course in bodybuilding. As soon as he had read through all the documents, he sent them an email: 'Dear Sir/Madam, I have now read through all your lessons. Please send me the muscles.' Believe it or not, many so-called 'spiritual aspirants' display a similar manner. And a little bit of humour can often go a long way. Serious issues can sometimes be better grasped with a sprinkling of humour. The mix of humour

i Taken from The Commanding Self (see Recommended Reading)

with a developmental path may involve a bit of give and take. Yet people usually act quite strange when it comes to the issue of negotiation or payment:

> *A person went to see a life coach to get some advice. 'Well,' began the coach, 'you must do this three times a week but never this…I wouldn't advise eating these things for your concentration but you can eat these…don't do this…but try doing the other but not too often…you must …' etc, etc, droned on the coach until the person eventually stood up and began to walk out. 'Hey,' called out the coach, 'you haven't paid me for my advice yet!' 'That's because I'm not taking it,' they replied back.*

The modern 'self-help' marketplace, to give it its lowest form, is like a buyer's market. Like all transactions, people pay and expect something in return. An eager student goes to visit a local well-known guitar teacher and asks how much it will cost to have private tuition. 'Well,' says the teacher. 'It will cost fifty dollars per hour for the first month of tuition. After that, it will be thirty dollars per hour.' 'Great,' replies the eager student, 'I'll start with the second month.'

Material in the form of humour is able to slip beyond the guardian of the 'Old Villain' – the complex of automatic thinking, conditioning, and assumptions which often regulate a person's lower perception. Humour and jokes have a way of being passed on, often veraciously, like a virus in the form of popular memes. Humour has a habit of going a long, long way. Humour disturbs our conditioning and annoys those people who prefer to adhere strictly to theirs. Hence, humour is often a good tool for testing the waters of flexibility, adaptability, and receptibility. Genuine developmental paths work with humour in one form or another, according to necessity.

One of the good things about humour is that its absence can be easily spotted. People without humour are easily identifiable. Yet real humour is not the slipping-on-banana-skin type of style. It is about how one views the world, and a point of observation that can step away from the norm. Banal, slapstick humour is more often associated with gurus than with genuine guides. Humour can be an accomplished instrument in showing up false situations or superficial behaviour. At the same time, it is often best not to explain just *how* the jokes and humour are used, as it detracts from its impact. Just like magicians don't like to reveal how the magic works as it would lose its appeal. The 'magic' of such a thing is in its impact upon the receiver – actually 'how' the process functions is a question of technicality.

Of course, it is often asked: 'how can jokes and such humour be developmental tools? Surely, they're just there to make us laugh?' Perhaps such people should just enjoy laughing and not concern themselves with oppositional behaviour. Unless, that is, they suffer from the widespread disease of 'I need to be confrontational.' It is also recognized that those people conditioned into certain ideologies often oppose most strongly the use of humour. I wonder how many people of 'faith' would find the following funny:

Three explorers – a priest, a businessman and a mystic – were passing through a dangerous jungle. As the journey continued the jungle became increasingly dangerous. As each day passed the animals appeared larger, more hostile, and eventually began to follow the three explorers.

Eventually the three explorers had to take refuge by climbing up a tree for fear they would be attacked. After convening a council to discuss the situation they decided that one of them

would have to go and seek help. After all, they could only stay up in the tree so many days before they succumbed to hunger, thirst, and fatigue. And none of the explorers wished to fall into the mouth of a ravenous beast below. But they could not decide which one of them should go.
'Not me,' said the priest. 'I am a servant of God and I need to stay behind to comfort the remaining person.

'Well, certainly not me,' said the businessman, 'because I am paying for the trip!'

The mystic said nothing, but then suddenly pushed the priest off from the tree. The priest fell to the ground. Immediately a ferocious pack of wolves surrounded the priest but instead of attacking him they defended him against the rest of the hungry animals. After fighting off the rest, they placed the priest on the back of their largest wolf and carefully escorted him to safety.

'It's a miracle!' cried the businessman. 'After all your cruelty, divine intervention decided to save that good man. And this has also restored my faith in a holy life.'

'Hold on, not so fast,' said the mystic. 'There is in fact another explanation for what you see.'

'What other explanation can there possibly be?' shouted the businessman angrily.

'Simply this – that it takes one to know one,' replied the mystic, 'and that the smallest always recognize their leader and honour him…'

Adopting beliefs can serve as a form of camouflage. It can be useful to check such conditioning by seeing whether certain humour can be endured.

Humour serves many different functions. Genuine developmental humour is an instrumental tool. It has various levels of meaning and receptivity. It does not operate solely to provide a single impact; although a single impact may only be perceived. A person may come to understand different aspects of a joke according to their mental or emotional state. Or it may require several exposures. How many times have we read a joke before we actually had the 'aha' effect? It may take the right moment. Our conditioned watchfulness may need to be caught off-guard.

Likewise, a person's reaction to a joke can tell a skilled observer many things about their state or perception. Jokes, if anything, are useful diagnostic tools. After all, a person may just not find certain jokes funny. Such as this one:

> *A tourist visits an ancient sacred temple in Asia. The guide, with great awe and reverence, is pointing out the various aspects of the sanctuary when they come to the alter. 'What's that?' asks the tourist, pointing to a light burning upon the alter. With a hushed voice the guide remarks that the flame has been burning for at least a thousand years. The tourist immediately steps forward and blows it out. 'Well, now it's stopped, hasn't it?'*

Immediate action is not always a person's preferred mode of behaviour. Others may prefer the more reflective route. Yet active or reflective, we are still beset by an abundance of assumptions. No more so than when it comes to a so-called 'spiritual path.' People tend to believe that a person of 'spirit' must act in ways that accord to certain individual or cultural values. Here's one take on this:

A western seeker-of-truth finally hears about a spiritual community where the aspirants neither eat meat nor smoke. Finally, they think to themselves, a place where they take such matters seriously. After all, eating meat means keeping animals in captivity, and which is also bad for environmental resources. Furthermore, smoking will only give you lung cancer. So off they go, and they gladly enrol into the centre. When they arrive into the main hall for lunch, they join all the other aspirants with their vegetable meals. Ah, they think, and such clean air too. Not a tobacco stain anywhere, and no dead-cooked animal carcass. Not surprisingly, even the older aspirants looked young and healthy. Later in the communal mediation hall they get to meet the Teacher of the community. Wow, thinks the new aspirant, this person doesn't look a day over fifty. Back at the dormitory the new aspirant asks another – 'How old is the Teacher? He looks so young!'

'Oh,' comes the reply, 'he's a hundred and twenty. I doubt any of us will ever reach such a venerable state. And he smokes twenty cigars a today and has fat, juicy steaks for breakfast, lunch, and dinner, now that he's past being affected by such frivolities that bind the rest of us.'

Sacrosanct opinions and beliefs can sometimes soon turn into sanctimonious ones. How often have we called someone pious when they were only exhibiting conditioned behaviour?

'A Pious Man'

'One day, an Imam called the people of Nasrudin's village together and delivered a sermon on the great deeds of the prophets. As he described the particularly noble achievements of one of these great men, Nasrudin suddenly burst into tears.

'Look at this pious man!' thundered the Imam. 'He is so moved that he weeps.'

'It's true,' sobbed the Mulla, 'you do reduce me to tears. My favourite goat died this morning and I miss him terribly. When you shake your head as you talk, your beard reminds me of my dead goat and I am moved to tears.'[1]

Good jokes are there to jolt the consciousness. They may also create a conflict with our conditioning.

In response to certain jokes we may not be sure whether to laugh or feign shock, knowing that companions, peers, or 'social norms' would expect of us that we be shocked. Sometimes a person may be afraid to laugh, thinking it will show others that they are disrespectful to this or that consensus custom. In modern times, there have been instances of 'social comedians' being harangued by the press, or even sued or taken to court over what is deemed 'unacceptable language' – meaning, they have offended certain social norms. A modern form of 'language censorship' has arisen to restrain particular freedoms of speech. In many cases, one is afraid of offending somebody in case of libel action. People may walk on tiptoes, but humour does not.

A western Christian missionary was kidnapped whilst visiting a remote tribal area. He was taken to the head tribe who, being cannibals, decided to eat the foreigner. They tied him up and put him in a large cooking pot and placed him over a low fire. Then the cannibals clasped their hands together and began to prey.

'Hey, hey,' shouted the man. 'You are Christians, you are Christians!'

'Yes,' replied the head tribesman. 'Not only are we Christians, we also do not like to be disturbed when we are praying!'

There is also a lot of unconscious humour present in daily life through circumstances and regular encounters. Life is funny in many ways, and not all of it predictable or recognizable.

Some jokes can present situations within a truthful light:

One day there was a mayor who decided that he could, and would, make all the inhabitants of his city observe the truth. He devised a plan that would make them all practice truthfulness. Now to enter the mayor's city you had to cross over a bridge. And upon this bridge the mayor built a hangman's gallows. Soon after, when all was complete, the city gates were re-opened, and the Captain of the Guard was stationed with a squad of troops to examine all who entered.
An announcement was made: 'Everyone will be questioned. If they tell the truth, they will be allowed to enter. If anyone lies, they will be hanged.
A simple farmer stepped forward.
'Where are you going and what is your business?'

'I am on my way to be hanged,' replied the farmer.
'We don't believe you!'
'Very well, if I have told a lie, hang me!'
'But if we hang you for lying,' replied the Captain of the Guard, 'we will have made what you said be the truth!'
'That's right: now you know what truth is – YOUR truth!'

Life itself can present us with humorous situations from which we can learn. Yet this does not mean that what is good for one's ordinary life is necessarily good for a developmental context. Whilst the two paths can – and indeed should – operate together harmoniously, the materials for one may not be appropriate for the other. Luck in life, as they say, may not bring luck in the other:

An oil-drilling millionaire went one day to his dentist in order to have some dental treatment.

'Which tooth is it you wish me to deal with today?' asked the dentist.
'Oh, drill away anywhere,' replied the oil tycoon, 'I feel lucky today.'

Having the materials in one's hands – such as a book – is no short-cut to an end result.

A lady was walking through her local country village carrying home some meat which she had just bought from the butcher. In her other hand she was holding a recipe for meat stew which her friend had just given to her after leaving the butchers. As she was about to reach her house a buzzard swooped down and carried off the meat.

'You fool!' shouted the lady. 'You may well have the meat, but I still have the recipe!'

Certain materials can provide the ingredients, yet a person still requires the knowledge of how to apply them – as well as the correct form of heat.

Applying the correct process requires active knowledge. As the saying goes - 'If you insist on buying poor food, you must be prepared to dislike it at the serving.' The 'food' that is put into the cooking (i.e., ourselves) will dictate the 'taste' (result) at the end of the cooking (developmental path). That is, we must be prepared to put in the correct effort ourselves – otherwise we may end up getting very wet!

A rich landowner one day invited one of his neighbours, a simple farmer, to go hunting with him and his friends. He thought it might be an amusing episode, and so gave the farmer a horse that was notoriously slow. The farmer noticed this immediately yet said nothing. Soon the hunt had begun, and the farmer was outpaced by all the faster horses. It then began to rain heavily and there was nowhere near enough to take shelter. All the members of the hunt got soaked through. The simple farmer, however, as soon as the rain started, had taken off all his clothes, folded them in a small, neat pile and sat on top of them. As soon as the rain stopped, he got dressed again and made his way to his host's house for lunch. Everybody else was wet through and couldn't understand how the farmer had arrived back seemingly dry. Despite the great speed of their horses, none of them had managed to reach the far shelter in time.

'It was the horse you gave me,' said the farmer when questioned.

The next time there was a hunt the farmer was invited again, and this time given a fast horse. The landowner decided that on this occasion he would take the reputedly slower horse. Again, a great rainstorm fell down and everyone got soaked through as before. Yet this time the landowner got wetter than ever, taking longer to arrive back home. The farmer, as previously, had done the same by sitting upon his folded pile of clothes. Upon returning to his host's house everyone was surprised to see him dry once more.

'Look at me, I'm drenched!' shouted the host, 'and it's all your fault. You made me ride that terrible horse!'

'Perhaps,' said the farmer, 'you did not contribute anything of your own to the problem of keeping dry?'

Social conditioning has been set-up to persuade people to place responsibility upon an external dependency. That is, some form of 'expert' will provide the needed result. This is also the same mentality that pervades most educational institutions. Parents pay money to send their children to school. They then complain when their child does not finish with a good result. It is assumed to be the school or teachers' fault. The same applies to how a developmental path is often measured:

A student had been attending a teaching group for several years. On a regular basis they had been attending the meetings and listening to the discourses of the teacher. After a number of years, however, the student began showing signs of restlessness. The teacher called the student in for a private talk.

'I have been giving you teachings and indications for a number of years now, and yet I fail to see any progress in you. This has started to concern me.'

'Ah, I'm glad you have finally noticed this,' replied the student, 'for I have been feeling for some months now that you are not trying hard enough!'

The modern seeker-of-truth is likely to suffer from varied assumptions upon what a developmental path should be. In fact, this has always been the case. Unlike other cultural manifestations, the perennial psychology has little interest in excitement and attention. It is unlikely to put on any shows, nor will there be any flashing neon signs around the neighbourhood. The signs that are available will be subtle. As the saying goes – 'A sign is enough for the alert, but a thousand counsels are not enough for the negligent.' It is often said that people should observe others as this can act as mirrors to recognize one's own behaviour. What they don't say in the same breath is that a mirror is also a means of laughing in your own face.

Upon the perennial path the importance of speaking with people according to their own understanding is well-recognized. As it is here:

A man had fallen onto the rails in an Underground station minutes before the next train was about to arrive. People were crowding around the man and trying to get him out. They were all shouting 'Give us your hand, give us your hand!' Yet the man would not reach up.

A student of the Path saw what was going on and made his way through the crowd. He called down to the man, asking 'Friend, what is your profession?'

'I am an income tax inspector,' cried out the man.

'In that case,' replied the student, 'take my hand!' The man immediately grasped the student's hand and was hauled up to safety.

The student turned to face the stunned onlookers. 'Never ask a tax man to **give** *you anything, you fools!' he said before walking away.*

The truth of the matter is that people need to experience things for themselves. Words can be spoken until 'we are blue in the face,' as the expression goes. Only through experience can a person know *how* to act in any given situation – such as in the case of the tax inspector above. The perennial tradition is about providing the means for the aspirant to undergo their own experience. A guide upon the Path serves to direct a person into an experience; or provide the means or context for the experience to occur. They cannot 'take the experience' for them – it would be like eating the food reserved for the other. Such methods do not provide nourishment for the seeker.

A teacher always told a parable at the end of each class, but not all the listeners would understand the meaning of it. One day one of them confronted the teacher and said:

'You tell us stories but do not explain the meaning to us.'

The teacher apologized for this and then continued by saying: 'Let me recompense you by offering you a juicy apple.'

'Thank you, teacher,' the student replied flattered.

'First, I would like to peel this apple myself, would you allow me?'

'Yes, thank you very much,' replied the delighted student.

'Since I already have a knife in my hand, let me take advantage of this and cut the apple into pieces so it will be more comfortable for you to eat.'

'Thank you, teacher, I hope it is not too much trouble?'

'Not at all, I just want to please you. Also, allow me to chew it before to make it easier for you to swallow.'

'No teacher - don't do that!' shrieked the surprised student.

The teacher paused and said:
'If I explain the meaning of each parable, it would be like feeding you a fruit chewed. You yourself have to find and savour its exquisite flavour. Only then will the fruit nourish you.'

Similarly, a father can teach their child how to ride a bike, for example, yet they cannot ride the bike for them. Unless a person acquires their own experience, they will not understand the context of the various circumstances that they are likely to come into contact with. This is why most perennial guides teach through *show* rather than *tell*, as in this tale:

A local guy made a wager with his friends that he could spend a whole winter's night on top of a nearby mountain without any form of shelter. His friends bet against him and laughed at his proposal. So, the young man took a book, and a candle to read, and sat through one of the coldest nights he had ever experienced. In the morning, freezing and almost half-dead, he arrived back down. He then went to collect the money from his bet with his friends.

'Didn't you have anything at all to keep you warm?' they asked.

'Nothing,' the young man replied.

'Not a blanket? A woolly hat?'

'Nope. Nothing.'

'Not even a candle?'

'Yes, I had a candle, so I could read.'

'Then the bet is off!' they cried.

The young man said nothing. Several weeks later he invited his friends around to his house for a huge supper. Everyone arrived and were excited at the prospect of the looming feast. They sat down and talked, waiting. Hours passed. Soon his friends started to mutter and get restless. They wanted to know when the food was coming.

'Let's go into the kitchen and have a look,' suggested the young man. Everyone followed him into the kitchen and there they found a huge pot under which a single candle was burning. The contents of the pot were still cold.

'It doesn't appear to be ready yet,' said the young man. 'Strange though, it's been there since yesterday.'

Without relevant and preparatory experience, all an aspiring seeker can expect to receive are the watered down, diluted versions of original truth. That is, a person may be feeding themselves upon second-hand news; or rather, upon the soup of the soup:

A farmer one day had one of his friends visit him from afar, and they brought a duck as a gift. The farmer was grateful and had the bird cooked and shared the meal with his guest.

Not long after another visitor arrived and said that he was a friend of the farmer's friend who had visited not long before. 'Remember,' said the visitor, 'the man who brought you the duck?' The farmer warmly invited the visitor in and fed him. Shortly afterwards another visitor arrived who said he was 'a friend of the friend of the one who brought the duck.'

This happened several times and the farmer's house soon became a point of reference for most of the visitors coming into town. Finally, the farmer was frustrated and annoyed. One day there was a knock at the door and it was another visitor who said, 'I am a friend of the friend of the friend of the friend of the man who brought you the duck.'

'Come in,' said the farmer. The visitor entered and sat himself down at the table to be fed. Shortly, the farmer brought a steaming bowl to the table and served his guest. When his guest tasted it, it seemed to be nothing more than hot water.

'What is this?' asked the guest.

'That,' replied the farmer, 'is the soup of the soup of the soup of the soup of the duck.'

The perennial tradition recognizes that the seeker is both the walker and the path. As such, each individual aspirant has sufficient resources within them to begin upon the journey:

A yokel went into a shop that stocked all kinds of materials and bits and pieces.
He asked the shop owner, 'Do you have any nails?'
'Yes,' said the owner.

'And leather – some good leather?'

'Yes, we have that too.'

'And thread – some good, strong thread?'

'Yes.'

'And dye?'

'Yes, we even have dye too.'

'Then why on earth don't you make yourself a pair of shoes?'

There is no excuse for not putting the first foot forward. Each individual can take the first step; after this though, they are likely to lack the wisdom and the understanding of *how to see* further along the path. For this reason, guides are placed on the Path for the seeker's benefit:

The village fool one day boasted to all who could hear that he could see in the dark.

'If that's so,' said one of the persons present, 'why is it that I've often seen you at night carrying a lighted torch through the streets?'

'Only to prevent other people from crashing into me,' the fool replied.

The perennial psychology is not directed at a particular section of society, for no such 'section' exists. It is directed at a certain faculty that exists within all people. The perennial tradition exists when this faculty is actualized, or 'awakened.' This path *is* human life itself.

As well as humorous tales and stories, the perennial psychology has also maintained a strong presence within literature; in many languages, and in almost all parts of the globe. Perennial wisdom has been present in some of the greatest known world literature.

References

[1] Shah, Idries. 2003. *The World of Nasrudin.* London: Octagon Press, p12.

Chapter Eight

ONCE UPON A TIME

'Every man who had ever lived became a contributor to the evolution of the earth, since his observations were a part of its growth. The world was thus a place entirely constructed from thought, ever changing, constantly renewing itself through the process of mankind's pondering its reality for themselves'

James Cowan – 'A Mapmaker's Dream'

'Stories emphasize the operations of divine immanence in the world'

Jonathan Black

Everyone reads stories or has read a story at one time or another. Stories make the world revolve and turn on its axis. Stories tell us about ourselves or show us *to* ourselves. We reflect upon our stories as well as being reflected in them. They are like constant companions that keep us company. They are also useful tools in learning how to be human. And yet, for the large part, they are underused. It is all too easy to miss the depth they can bring to us. Like a lazy lover, we miss the mark in seeing the true beauty looking back.

Even though society educates people, it also conditions us to interpret stories through associative methods or logical reasoning. People are also accustomed to responding to emotional content, and from this they often feel they have 'gained' something due to an emotional satisfaction. In these instances, people are being fed by the story but not nurtured. There is a difference. And there is also a difference between regular, worldly literature and what is known as 'instrumental' literature.

It is not so easy to break away from trained responses. Many people have been taught that it is 'noble' and 'good' to have emotional responses to art and literature. Unknowingly, people have allowed themselves into being triggered in predictable ways. This 'triggering' is also a science that has crept into recent propaganda and marketing exercises. To be 'emotionally impacted' is, we are told, to feel a human connection with the world. In fact, it is an exercise in attachment to external impulses which people are trained to internalize and to 'make our own.' On the other hand, from early schooldays we have been taught to be analytical and to extract information in an overly associative and intellectual way. This too is a limited form of understanding which keeps greater truths at bay.

There have been a significant number of developmental texts that were constructed in a deliberate manner to oppose a rational and sequential approach. Their purpose is to affect a change in the reader's perception in order to trigger an altered comprehension of reality. Such works aim for a comprehensive and integral understanding. It is not the aim here to make a list of these works. They are, however, scattered throughout existing literature and can be spotted by the attentive reader.

Stories and material that belong to a developmental path, and to the perennial tradition specifically, are often referred to as 'instrumental.' These materials function upon different and varying levels. The intellectual and emotional content of stories may be likened to the common senses of sight and smell - just as an apple has the sight and smell of an apple. Yet the sight and smell do not provide the nutritional value – the nourishment – of the apple. Only when an apple is 'tasted' can these values be experienced and absorbed. Most stories function upon the sight and smell level only, and in general this can be sufficient. Yet materials for a developmental path must provide nutrients, otherwise they will become mechanical. Similarly, when a person responds by saying something like – 'I really felt moved by this' – then the response too shows a level of automatism. Human perception can be developed by gradually observing *how* certain stimuli impacts us, and to carefully monitor internal responses.

Writings that belong to the perennial psychology are primarily instrumental before they are meant for entertainment, enjoyment, or emotional stimulation. However, they can also be taken on these levels, for they assist in its cultural transmission and longevity. The literary and entertainment value of stories allows for their continued use and survival as they are not dependent upon time-restricted cultural norms. The aim of such instrumental literature is to connect with a part of the individual which cannot be reached by conventional means. Elements can be communicated in a way that is not blocked by conditioning or similar cultural limitations.

Instrumental writings are aimed at seeding specific concepts and ideas ahead of their actual realization. That is, they work to prepare the human mind for developmental processes. They can be referred to as a form of 'spiritual technology.' Instrumental writings of this type can be found within almost all forms of literature from around the world, in all epochs, from Persian poets to English playwrights. For the main body of this chapter, I will refer to two major historical figures of literature – Jallaludin Rumi and William

Shakespeare.[i] These figures are just the tip of the iceberg, as they say, yet they represent the continuation of the perennial tradition from two epochs and continents.

Instrumental literature often provides allegorical descriptions of experiences that are said to lead a person from their ordinary state to higher states. Experiences associated with higher states are all but invisible to the ordinary person. That is why such literature contains various levels of exterior and interior meaning. The literature is itself 'experienced' according to the state of the reader/listener. The ordinary intellect may grasp the first layer of meaning. Subsequent levels, however, remain beyond the grasp of the rational and conditioned mind. As Rumi states in his major work the Mathnawi -

> From his present state, man needs to continue his migration so that he may escape from his rationality and intellectuality which are driven mostly by greed and egotism. There are a hundred thousand more marvelous states ahead of him. He fell asleep and became oblivious of the past. This world is the sleeper's dream and the sleeper's fancies. (Book IV, 3637-3667)[ii]

---

i For more information on the confluence of these two historical figures, see - Shakespeare's Sequel to Rumi's Teaching by Wes Jamroz (see Recommended Reading)

ii All quotes taken from Rumi's Mathnawi are referenced according the Reynold A. Nicholson translation – The Mathnawi of Jalaluddin Rumi (Books I-VI), Edited and Translated by Reynold A. Nicholson (The E.J.W. Gibb Memorial Trust, 1982)

The world is the 'sleeper's dream' because people, in general, have become disconnected from a source of wisdom, and thus from experiencing 'direct Reality.' Within this dislocation a person falls back onto rationality and intellectuality – the conditioned trappings of a lower state. When in such a state, a person is liable to only grasp the first, outer layer of meaning within instrumental literature when in fact multiple layers exist.

These two conditions, of being awakened or asleep to the higher states of perception, were illustrated in Shakespeare's famous 'to be or not to be' soliloquy in Hamlet –

> To be, or not to be--that is the question:
> Whether 'tis nobler in the mind to suffer
> The slings and arrows of outrageous fortune
> Or to take arms against a sea of troubles
> And by opposing end them? (Hamlet, III.1)

The state of 'not to be' is a non-developmental state. It can be said that this is the state of ordinary being. It is under the influence of life's normal impacts – 'The slings and arrows of outrageous fortune' – which is the lot suffered by most people in the world. Whereas the state 'to be' corresponds to a person of inner development. This path is one that leads to the eventual activation of inner faculties that can perceive higher truth. This path requires a personal struggle against worldly, lower forces – 'to take arms against a sea of troubles/And by opposing end them.'

Perennial developmental literature often shows these opposing conditions between the 'ordinary' state and the state of 'spiritual' or inner activation. Also, such instrumental literature indicates when a stage of development may be in process, or the conditions for its emergence. The perennial tradition manifests in new forms at a specific time and place as part of an operational new phase in the developmental path. At such times, previously prescribed techniques are superseded and must be abandoned. Many tales in literature have told of false idols and how they consume their practitioners who are blind to the need to let go and move on. Such people are consumed by their own fixations. The genuine path is one of continued flexibility and attunement to current needs, according to time and place.

Those people fixated with their own ideas of what is true and what is not have been corrupted by a false personality. It is these conditionings, as previously discussed, which need to be released. If not, they may eventually consume and destroy the person. Spiritual death at the hands of one's own false self is depicted in the famous fable of the lion who dominates the jungle and all its inhabitants. The lion is finally persuaded that his dominance is under threat from another lion in the jungle. He is led to a pond (or a well) and told to look within. Upon seeing his reflection, the lion believes he is being confronted by the face of another lion. In anger he leaps into the water, only to be consumed and drowned. Similar variations upon this theme have been found in Aesop's fables as well as variants around the world. Such fables are a rich source of instrumental guidance and have formed a core stream of perennial wisdom throughout the ages.

Similarly, there is the tale that tells of a great King[iii] who organized an expedition to find the Water of Eternal Life. After long journeys, the King finally found the cave where the spring of life was gushing forth. He entered the

iii Some versions attribute this tale to Alexander the Great.

cave with great anticipation and rushed forward to drink from the water. As he stooped down to drink, he heard a strange sound above him. Upon looking up he saw what appeared to be a crow perched in the darkness. 'Stop – whatever you do, don't drink the water!' screeched the crow. 'Why shouldn't I?' replied the King. 'I have taken great troubles to reach this place – surely I am deserving?' The crow answered – 'Great King, take a look at me. I too sought out the water of life and drank from it. Now, a thousand years later, without the sight of any eye, with my beak broken, my claws rotten and fallen off, and not even a feather left to clothe my body – all I ask for now is the impossible: I ask TO DIE, yet I cannot.' The great King, realizing that a true aim must be articulated in accordance with knowledge and not just desire, stood up and hurried away from the Water of Life.

The aspirant upon the true path must be released from the conditioned fixations of desire. In order to be released from such fixations, a person is required to undertake the process known as 'to die before you die.' This refers to a dying (release) from the false self. This knowledge often has to be transmitted indirectly, through analogy or through certain 'behaviour' to those who are ready to receive. There is a famous tale from Rumi's Mathnawi called 'The Merchant and his Parrot' that reflects this. In a modern translation it is given as:

> *There was a certain merchant who kept a parrot in a cage. Being about to travel to a far country on business, he asked the parrot if he had any message to send to his kinsmen in that country. The parrot thought for a while and finally told the merchant to inform his kinsmen that he was kept confined in a cage.*

The merchant promised to deliver this message, and on reaching the far country, and finding a flock of parrots, he recited the message as it had been given to him. On hearing it one of the parrots immediately fell down dead. The merchant was annoyed with his own parrot for having sent such a fatal message, and upon his return home he sharply rebuked his parrot for doing so. But the parrot no sooner heard the merchant's story than he too fell down dead in his cage.

The merchant, after lamenting his death, took the parrot's body out of the cage and threw it away; but, to his surprise, the parrot immediately recovered life, and flew away. The parrot then explained that the fellow parrot from the far country had only feigned death to suggest this way of escaping from confinement in a cage.

Feigning death (death of the false self) is shown as a method of release from worldly captivity (confinement in a cage). A person who is captive to the material reality (the lower world) will not be able to receive more subtle impacts. One must first 'die' to the conditionings that bind one to a lower realm of perception.

The ordinary person, however, is generally absorbed with satisfying the false self. This false, or deceiving, self is often compared in perennial literature to that of a beast. In some tales and anecdotes, it is represented as a beast that is carrying a person upon a journey. That is, the inner self is being carried – or 'taken for a ride' – by the false self. In these tales it is suggested that the beast (ass, donkey, mule, etc.) delivers the person to their destination but then the person is required to dismount if they wish to go further. One well-known eastern proverb states this as – 'You may ride a donkey to your front door, but would you ride it into your house?'

The sets of beliefs and understanding that ordinary people surround themselves with become the barriers and obstacles towards any further development. Often a guide – a teaching – is needed to act as an intervention. This process of intervention is seldom recognized, or accepted, as necessary by an ordinary person, or even by a would-be student. This tale shows how an outside intervention from a person of knowledge is necessary:

An intelligent man was riding out on his horse one day through the countryside when he spotted the figure of someone sleeping. As he rode closer he saw what appeared to be a drunken person sleeping and snoring loudly under a tree. As he watched he also saw that a snake crawled down from the branches of the tree and entered into the mouth of the sleeping man.

Immediately the rider rode up, jumped off his horse and took his riding whip against the sleeping fellow. The man awoke with a howl of pain. He was confused and couldn't understand why someone would do such a thing.

'Get up and run, you fool!' shouted the rider.

The drowsy man climbed to his feet and began to stagger. The rider continued to whip the man to make him run faster. He followed the man, whipping him all the time, until they came to a nearby tree where many rotten apples had fallen to the floor. The rider demanded that the drunken man eat as many rotten apples as he could. He whipped him several times into obedience. The man ate out of fear, not knowing why someone would want to do such a thing to him. He pleaded to the rider, yet to no avail.

'Cruel stranger, let a poor man be. I have done nothing to you,' he pleaded.

The rider did not listen and only whipped him harder. 'Now run, faster!' he shouted.

The man continued to run around the field as he was chased and whipped by the rider until eventually, through exhaustion and all the rotten apples in his stomach, he fell down upon his knees and vomited. All of a sudden, a snake came out of him and slipped hurriedly away into the underbrush.

Then the man realized what had happened.

'If I had told you there was a snake inside you,' said the rider, 'you would have either thought I was lying and ignored me or become immobilized by shock. Both these actions could have killed you. There was no alternative but to do what I did, unbeknown to you.'

The man knew then that the rider had perceived a greater truth unavailable to him; and he was thankful for it.

Shakespeare tells of a similar experience in *Taming of the Shrew* in the description of Petruchio's treatment of Katharina in waking her from her 'sleep' –

> 'In her chamber, making a sermon of continency to her;
> And rails, and swears, and rates, that she, poor soul,
> Knows not which way to stand, to look, to speak,
> And sits as one new-risen from a dream.' (IV.1)

What these and other tales are showing is that there are two types of knowing; that is, two ways of accessing knowledge. The ordinary person deals with conventional knowledge that comes mainly through external sources. The person of inner development is nourished from an objective knowledge that is received through a faculty of perception (often referred to as intuition). Rumi clearly indicates this in the following poem:

Two Kinds of Intelligence

There are two kinds of intelligence: One acquired,
as a child in school memorizes facts and concepts
from books and from what the teacher says,
collecting information from the traditional sciences
as well as from the new sciences.

With such intelligence you rise in the world.
You get ranked ahead or behind others
in regard to your competence in retaining
information. You stroll with this intelligence
in and out of fields of knowledge, getting always more
marks on your preserving tablets.

There is another kind of tablet, one
already completed and preserved inside you.
A spring overflowing its springbox. A freshness
in the center of the chest. This other intelligence
does not turn yellow or stagnate. It's fluid,
and it doesn't move from outside to inside
through the conduits of plumbing-learning.

This second knowing is a fountainhead
from within you, moving out.[iv]

The shift from one stage or state to another – such as from ordinary knowledge to perceiving inner, direct knowledge – is often depicted in various tales using the motif of transformation.

Perhaps the most famous use of this motif is the transformation from the ugly duckling to the swan in the Hans Christian Anderson tale that is a firm children's favourite. This 'alchemical' transformation suggests a state-shift from a raw to a more developed stage. Another well-known example of this shift is in Shakespeare's historical play *Henry IV* regarding the young prince Harry who, as a young man, leads a wild and hedonistic lifestyle – in taverns and with shady friends. His father despairs of him. Yet the young prince seems aware that he is experiencing the preparatory stage, until he is called upon to step up to his function. Upon his father's death the young prince makes a sudden and radical change in himself. At this point he abandons his closest 'friend'the character Falstaff - as he leaves behind his earlier, lowly state with the now-famous words: 'I know thee not, old man; fall to thy prayers; How ill white hairs become a fool and jester!' (Henry IV – Pt2, V.5).

In terms of the developmental process, perennial literature has often made mention of three types of persons. These may symbolically be described as the 'wise person,' the 'half-wise' person, and the 'stupid' person. The wise person is invariably the Guide, the one who knows the way. The 'half-wise' person is the one who is awake enough to

iv Originally from Mathnawi IV:1960-1968 – modern translation by Coleman Barks.

be able to recognize the existence of the guide and their function. And the 'stupid' person is the blind one who relies upon their own conditioned emotions and beliefs and refuses to acknowledge or accept the existence of the guide. This form is illustrated in the tale of the three fishes that appears in the Mathnawi:

> *There was in a secluded place a lake, which was fed by a running stream. In this lake were three fishes; the wise, the half-wise, and the foolish one. One day some fishermen passed by that lake and having espied the fish hastened home to fetch their nets. The fish also saw the fishermen and were greatly disquieted. The wise fish said, 'I will not debate with the others, for assuredly they will dispute with me. And there is no time for arguments and persuasion. They love their native place so much that they will not be ready to come with me.' Without any delay the wise fish left the lake and took refuge in the running stream, which was linked to it. In this way he escaped the impending danger. The half-wise fish delayed doing anything till the fishermen returned and threw their nets. The half-wise fish was quite distressed. He said, 'I have lost the opportunity! Why did I not follow the guide? He has gone towards the sea and is freed from sorrow. Such a good comrade has been lost to me! But I will not think of that and will attend to free myself. I will become dead. I will turn my belly upwards and will commit myself to the water. To die before death is to be safe from torment.' So he floated upon the surface of the water, pretending to be dead. A fisherman seized him and flung him on the ground. The half-wise fish, rolling over and over, managed to jump into the stream. In this way he gained his freedom. The foolish fish remained where he was, moving to and fro in agitation. That simpleton kept leaping about, right and left, in order that he*

might save himself by his own efforts. He was easily caught and killed by the fishermen. (Book IV, 2188-2300)

The aspirant cannot save themselves by their own efforts if such efforts are not guided by a minimal quota of knowledge or awareness. A similar state of affairs is symbolized in the form of the three men in Shakespeare's *The Merchant of Venice* who intend to marry Portia (who symbolically is the guide). Each of the men must pass their own trial in order to woo Portia. Each aspirant (suiter) displays their state of awareness through their subsequent actions.

A person who enters upon a developmental path will be required to go through a range of experiences that are likened to trials, in order to test various capacities. These trials usually expose a person to a spectrum of experiences from which they can learn. Many tales, ranging from within most if not all cultures, tell of the 'hero's journey' through such a series of trials – from Jason of the Argonauts; to Odysseus; to Pericles, Prince of Tyre. This phase of the developmental path toward activation of higher states through a range of trials and experiences is often symbolically described as a journey or quest. In various forms of instrumental literature, it has been represented as a lover's quest, the search for treasure, or indeed as the search for destiny or truth. Similarly, the entire series of Shakespeare's History Plays can be seen as an illustration of the transformative process that gradually leads to the development of a true human 'King.' (v

Likewise, in perennial literature the unitive (love) energy is symbolically compared to wine. Its effect upon human consciousness is likened to drunkenness. Spiritual

v For more information, see the *Shakespeare for the Seeker* series of books by Wes Jamroz (Troubadour Publications).

drunkenness, however, is only an intermediate step and not the objective. Hence, drinking and inebriation is required up to a certain point, at which time the person needs to abandon this stage if they are to progress further. Similarly, the term/image of the cupbearer refers to a spiritual guide (i.e., the keeper of the wine), and to be able to give a full cup of wine symbolizes the guide's capacity to fill an aspirant's heart with unitive energy (love). Many eastern poems deal with the theme of wine and intoxication – the most famous being the quatrains of Omar Khayyam.[vi] Similarly, many references also occur in western literature of cupbearers presenting the King/Queen with wine (especially in Late Middle Age and Jacobean literature). The aspirant's heroic journey is said to end in the lover's meeting – the reception of the unitive love energy. Shakespeare used the Fool in *Twelfth Night* to express this as – 'Journeys end in lovers meeting,/Every wise man's son doth know.' (II.3)
Similarly, Rumi expressed the journey's end as – 'Unless you gain possession of the candle, there is no path. But when you have embarked upon the path, your path becomes the journey. And when you have reached the journey's end, you meet the Truth.'

To 'meet the Truth' requires that first the process of inner development (the hero's journey) leads to the formation of a new 'organ' of perception. This organ of supracognitive perception allows the human to act in accordance with the grander scheme. It is a perception that transcends ordinary space-time limitations. This 'level' of perception is referenced in the following short tale:

---

vi The author would not recommend the popularist translations of Edward FitzGerald. Instead he would point the interested reader toward the controversial 1967 translation by Robert Graves and Omar Ali-Shah.

> *One day a mule was placed in a desert stable where he met a camel. The mule said to the camel –*
>
> *'How is it that you camels never fall down in the sand? We mules are always stumbling and falling down whereas you don't seem to ever make a wrong step.'*
>
> *The camel replied, 'Our eyes are always directed upwards. We see far into the distance and know what is coming a long time before it arrives. Whereas you only look down and observe what is immediately beneath your feet.'*

The operation of subtle faculties is an experience beyond normal senses – beyond the regular senses of touch, taste and smell. The activation of the subtle faculties is one stage in the inner development of a person. This is followed by the fusion of these new faculties as they form a more permanent state of inner being. This can be likened to the famous tale of the elephant in the dark room, whereby ordinary people are not able to perceive beyond their limited regular senses the fusion of the parts into an emergent inner being (in this case, the whole elephant). When a person has developed their inner faculties (the 'subtle' faculties), every act they make has constructive purpose. That is, they act in accordance with a greater plan. As such, their behaviour cannot be judged from the standpoint of the ordinary person, who is incapable of perceiving the 'correctness' of such acts.

The image of the peacock is often used in perennial literature to refer to vanity. As Rumi states – 'Do not admire your peacock-feathers but look at his ugly feet, so that your vanity may not lead you astray.' The peacock symbolizes a person who attaches too much importance to worldly affairs, which blocks evolutionary development. Such worldly attractions are often related to the peacock's plumage. The aspiring seeker is in need of learning 'proper conduct.'

The term 'proper conduct' is a technical term in developmental literature that refers to a process that leads to the unveiling, or activation, of higher inner states. The term 'proper conduct' does not refer to behaviour in line with social norms, customs, or rituals. This behaviour may be socially laudable – or an act of imitation – yet it remains far from the realm of the inner path. Rather, it refers to acts that correspond with an inner knowing that lead to the activation of higher faculties within a person.

Perennial instrumental literature is a consciously constructed vehicle that operates on multiple levels. It survives because it also serves a social need and has cultural value. That is, it can also provide entertainment value. This is its sheath. Unbeknownst to most people, a stream of wisdom has flowed, and continues to flow, through many and varied cultures. Some of the most valued and prized literature and tales are offerings of developmental instruction. And yet the perennial tradition remains a secret that protects itself. The astute person is urged to perceive through the veil that maintains the ghostly illusion of ordinary reality.

Chapter Nine

GIVING UP THE GHOST
(A GNOSTIC VISION)

'I lived in this world of darkness for myriads of years and no one ever knew that I was there.'

Gnostic Hymn

'If you bring forth what is within you, what you bring forth will save you. If you do not bring forth what is within you, what you do not bring forth will destroy you.'

Gospel of Thomas

The perennial tradition has also been referred to at various times as a gnostic path. Many commentators view Gnosticism as referring to a system of religious beliefs that emerged in the early centuries of the common era (around 1st and 2nd century C.E.). These ideas flourished widely around the Mediterranean regions in these times and synthesized in many and various groupings and sects. Whilst these semi-religious groupings shared some core ideas they diverged into competing systems of cosmic and religious-spiritual hierarchies. Gnostic elements also found their way into the western renaissance, and many researchers have noted their Platonic, Neo-Platonic, and Persian influences. As stated previously, genuine wisdom streams inevitably crystalize into outward forms and structures. With time, these structures cease to be vitalized and updated with living content. Hence, the perennial psychology has 'travelled' within the Gnostic path. In this case, it is Gnosticism and yet it is not.

Gnosis is a term that signifies the direct perception of knowledge. In this sense, gnosis is very much at the heart of the perennial path. Gnostic insight gave rise to some of the ideas, concepts, and philosophies that developed into the more structured thought of Gnosticism. It is valid for the discussion here of the perennial tradition to delve, albeit briefly, into some of these gnostic concepts. This is especially relevant for modern times as many of these ideas and concepts are percolating through contemporary cultures. As I shall show, some of the most popular recent films are treatments of gnostic themes. In a world of increasing materiality, the gnostic vision is as pertinent as ever.

As stated, gnosis refers to a direct perception of the greater Truth. It offers an expression of a particular knowledge of reality. This knowledge ultimately transforms the human psyche and heightens the perceptual faculties. In its essence, it is developmental knowledge arrived at intuitively. It is perennial because intuitive truth is not changed by time, place, or the people who perceive it. It is, has been, and always will be. It is only the outer manifestations and expressions of this truth that vary. The perennial gnosis develops a distinct consciousness within a person that gives them a new permanence to their cognition and thus actions. The person is then able to see through the falsehoods associated with ordinary, consensus reality. This position allows them to seek liberation from the 'shackles' of this world. Put simply, perennial gnosis is a quest for a new type of consciousness within the human that modifies perception of knowledge in relation to a higher truth and reality. Such knowledge is contingent with the present moment and has no place in the past. It is a living knowledge that fills the shape of the container into which it is poured. Gnosis liberates the human being from its state of inner infancy.

The perennial gnostic path is a chain of transmission rather than an enduring form. This transmission can provide knowledge about the structure of reality. Or rather, it provides the means whereby a person may approach Truth/Reality themselves. It is not a system, yet it exists as a systematic body of knowledge. And this chain of transmission has also existed at all times and continues to exist in contemporary cultures today. Gnosis is a specific perception vis-à-vis Reality. It provides direct experience that is beyond all forms of secondary perception or cultural systems of knowledge. The experience of the Real triggers an awakening of a specific impulse, or faculty, within the person. This inner impulse can be said to be the source of inner revelations and vision. There is a component within each person that can be activated. For the most part, this component remains within a state of semi-latency, awaiting certain impulses. Within this state of semi-latency, it still attempts to communicate through symbols, dreams, synchronicities, and non-verbal means. For further development it requires an active participation from the person. The symbols given out by this inner component can reveal a path of psychological development towards awakening. The gnostic side of the perennial psychology recognizes that some people are able to 'auto-activate' their developmental potential. Within each person resides a residual memory of wholeness. That is why the perennial gnostic path emphasizes the state of dormancy – the 'fallen state' of humanity.

The gnostic path recognizes that psychological development is not an easy task for we are surrounded by forces that seek to dominate this 'fallen' state. Such forces seek to compel us with foolish thoughts and behaviour. People are imbued with unconscious compulsions that act against their developmental potential. These forces have been given many names over the years, which shall not be dwelt further upon here. It is each person's responsibility to overcome these negative forces. Unless a person can release themselves from such negative influences, the perennial path will always be blocked to them. Ordinary life renders a person under the dominant sway of incompatible forces.

Perennial gnosis perceives these degenerative impulses at work. The developmental path recognizes that there exist forces of 'psychic impoverishment.' This recognition is especially important for the contemporary world, for such forces are not only active now as ever, yet more visible in their machinations. When people lack sufficient psychological insight, they are open and vulnerable to such oppressive and degenerative impulses. Unawareness of these forces can bring about emotional, mental, and physical destabilization. The perennial psychology does not regard this as being pessimistic but rather as a necessary and functional insight toward inner liberation. Human life is a process of 'soul-making' (as discussed in Chapter One). Those persons who identify with the physical-material world to the exclusion of their psychic-inner natures have allowed the physical world to render them as 'dead inside.' That is why there is frequent mention in wisdom traditions about death, dying, and journeys into the underworld.

As human beings, we not only have responsibility to the external world but also to the interior world – the individual's inner life. The perennial tradition shows that a person cannot truly live by the conventions of society alone or from the impacts of everyday life. People also need sustenance from the source that is beyond all social institutions, and from beyond physical life itself. No healthy tree can disown its own roots that grow deep into the dark soil below. To do so would bring death. The human being is rooted in its own soils too.

In order to achieve permanent change, a person must develop themselves from within, not just changing their ideas. In the Gospel of Thomas, it is said: 'There is light within a man of light, and it lights up the whole world. If he does not shine, there is darkness.' The perennial gnostic path opposes the sense of meaningless in life and reaches for correspondence with the essential. Such meaning cannot be given but must be lived and experienced. The living of such meaning is a mysterious process that is revealed also through the power of myth, dreams, and the imagination.

An individual may not be free to choose their destiny, yet they are free to choose whether they wish for gnosis and genuine knowledge of Reality or not. A person who chooses to become an aspirant upon the perennial path needs to make enough personal effort to gain sufficient self-awareness to break away from a state of conditioned ignorance. Gnostic perception is a true awareness of oneself and of one's destiny and place in the universe. First, however, one must recognize that ordinary life is as if living within a veil of illusion.

The Veil of Illusion

The inner reality is real. People are conditioned into thinking that 'psychic' elements are inferior to the physical things of life because they are 'non-material.' Modern societies, especially, neglect or ignore completely the power of psychic phenomenon. The unfortunate result of this is that humanity, by and large, is oppressed by forces that dominate and suppress inner impulses and developmental faculties. What many people are experiencing today is the moral uncertainty that precedes a new understanding, as the old patterns of thought cease to be adequate for a new phase of human development.

Human enterprises and institutions – those systems of power, social management, political bodies, etc. – are naturally flawed by human design. They operate and function through processes that sustain a view of reality that is limited. In some cases, this is a deliberate act. The world in which humans live is a machination of unrealized desires, emotions, and unenlightened agendas. However, within this opaqueness lies immense potential for the light to enter. The human psyche must recognize the need to filter the negative influences of this world and refine them. As long as the majority of people expect all problems to be solved outside of themselves, human societies will continue to be dominated by unruly forces. Liberation from these forces depends upon people willing to assume the responsibility of consciousness, and to project this inner reality outwards upon an external environment. In the words of one commentator: 'man is called upon, in this struggle against the generalized oppressiveness of the real, to create a soul for himself, or if you prefer, to nourish, fortify, and enrich the luminous spark he carries in his innermost being.'[1]

Activating and enriching the luminous spark is part of the process of the perennial tradition. That is the great perennial task: to become what we have always been, and to show others the way through our own individual presence and behaviour. Through our deliberate and conscious presence, we can assist others to become what they have always been also.

The situation as presented from a gnostic viewpoint – as living within a reality that is an illusory one – is becoming more prevalent within modern cinema. The 'gnostic memes' – or rather, perennial codes – have been transmitted in an array of films; especially so in the past few decades. The following are examples, although there have been many more: *Total Recall* (1990 – remade 2012); *Pleasantville* (1998); *Dark City* (1998); *The Truman Show* (1998); *eXistenZ* (1999); *The Thirteenth Floor* (1999); *The Matrix* (1999), *Donnie Darko* (2001); *Vanilla Sky* (2001), *Cloud Atlas* (2012); *Doctor Strange* (2016); and *Ghost in the Shell* (2017).

Films with a gnostic element often show ambiguous relationships between humans and other intelligences; reality and dream fantasy; the interior psyche and material reality; evil and the angelic impulse. And through these dualistic struggles there is the underlying sense that despite the commercial core of Hollywood there is also something else - something almost otherworldly and unknowable - lurking within. These celluloid projections transmit a vague feeling that something isn't quite right, and this makes the viewer question their own sense of reality. Such gnostic visions not only unravel the falsity of the external world but also point towards the potential for finding transcendence; or of breaking through the veil of illusion.

One of the most entertaining and accurate portrayals of the gnostic vision in cinema in recent years is *The Truman Show* (1998). Directed by Peter Weir and written by Andrew Niccol, this popular film will be known to many readers. It tells the story of the character Truman Burbank (played by Jim Carrey) whose life is a live reality show, unbeknown to him. The television producer named Christof (played by Ed Harris) is the Gnostic demiurge – or false god - who has created an artificial world: a huge domed town with computer-controlled weather patterns, fake sky and sea, and populated by actors playing their scripted parts. He has created a simulated world where everything *seems* to be true but is not. We know this because we are the 'viewers' outside, looking in (we are in fact the viewers of the viewers of the drama). The principle character of Truman Burbank is ignorant of his condition and of the nature of his world - to him everything is real. His life has been created (manipulated) to exist as a character in his own television show. He is watched 24/7, fed false information, and his dreams are constantly dashed or talked down by those around him. He lives in an unseen prison from which he is unable to escape for he does not consider escape a necessity. The character of Truman is both a willing prisoner of his false reality as well as a manipulated prisoner by those external to his reality. And yet, as is central to the gnostic vision, something eventually triggers Truman - he falls in love.

Truman (true man) notices the beautiful Sylvia (played by Natascha McElhone) who from afar attracts him with her presence. Because she is just a vision to him, someone he has yet to meet, she exists outside of his everyday mundane, tangible material existence. He sees, recognizes, something in her that provides him with a vision, and this ultimately becomes his liberating catalyst. After she is taken away from him (to leave the show forever) for breaking the 'game rules,' Truman is motivated to leave his old world - to seek his beloved (the archetypal Gnostic quest). Yet this longing within him creates a feeling of melancholy (detachment from the Real). It is through this melancholy that Truman begins to notice things he hadn't recognized before - the same people saying the same things at precisely the same time, and odd anomalies appearing in his 'reality.' In other words, he has been triggered into awareness, and now he is able to see his world from a different perspective. His eventual planned escape culminates in an almost mythical voyage across the sea. Despite his conditioned fear of water, he plunges himself into the abyss. He shows that he is ready to die, to sacrifice himself, in order to secure his liberation. In perennial terms, he is ready to 'die before you die' in order to shed his old life. Finally, he reaches the 'end' of his world and arrives at the door (portal) to what is for him another reality. Yet before he leaves his old world the voice of Christof - his 'creator god'addresses him in a soft voice. He tells Truman that he is safer within this world; that he is protected and loved. 'Was nothing real?' asks Truman. Christof replies that he, Truman, was real. And that since there are lies and deceit on both sides, there is no difference, and thus he would be better to choose the sanctuary of security over the unknown. Truman, now knowing the false reality in which he lives, decides that the truth is a price worth paying for. He takes a bow and leaves the stage.

The camera then shifts to scenes of millions of people all over the world watching blank, static screens as the real-time live feed is cut. Their ongoing addictive dose of reality TV has been cut off. The last viewers shown are two parking garage attendants who seem stunned at first. Then they reach for another piece of pizza and turn over the channel to see what else might be on television to watch. As the film finishes, what do *we* do? We leave the cinema or turn off the television and go and do something else. Everything is just television, an enjoyable piece of entertainment. It's not real. And then we go about our business as usual, as if our own scripts have been written. Yet those of us who watched the film have been the real viewers all along, and this is the gnostic twist.

As the viewer turns away from the film, they may ask themselves – was anything recognized within *The Truman Show* that reflects our own existence? Once triggered into awareness, the person is then confronted with a similar dilemma that faced Truman. Should you continue with your old life knowing that it is all a grand illusion, a false reality? Or are you willing to take the plunge into the abyss and be willing to 'die before you die' in order to find the truth? Does the individual have the urge, the drive, which motivated Truman to finally reject the comfort and security offered to him by his 'creator'? Could any of us make that decision to walk through the door and to throw away all that we have known in our lives? Truman – the 'true man' – did, and he reached his goal.

The Truman Show could be said to have parallels with the ancient Gnostic tale of 'The Precious Jewel,' as was told in Chapter One. The heart of gnostic understanding shows that the first move must come from within each person. The individual may not always find the goal by seeking, and yet seeking is the first condition required. Few are those that realize that there exists the possibility for a developmental path toward a level of perception beyond the current state. It is through the here and now of the material world that a genuine seeker is forced to operate.

As already noted, the perennial tradition does not attempt to missionize or to convince people of its presence or its truth. It does not need to. It is down to each person to convince themselves whether they are sincere and genuine in their seeking. Everything comes back to the individual. This knowledge cannot be gained or understood unless a person first makes some corresponding room for it within them. To repeat - the seeker is both the walker and the path. And one of the first steps to be taken is to recognize that the dominant view of the world is only a description of a limited reality. As the mystic Iskandar of Balkh once proclaimed – 'You shall become aware, through daily practice, that what you imagine to be your self is concocted from beliefs put into you by others, and is not your self at all.'

Only by realizing that the mind's eye is blind can one begin to gain the first slither of sight. Until the seeker can feel this longing for the genuine inner life within, then they remain attracted, like the moth, to the larger flame offered by the distractions of the external world. These distractions are sometimes useful – they can also be necessary – yet it is important to recognize them for what they are. They are part of the 'game of life' that is played in this reality. It is vital to know how to play the game.

References

[1] Lacarriere, Jacques. 1977. *The Gnostics*. London: Peter Owen, p50.

Chapter Ten

PLAYING THE GAME

'False teachers and deceived seekers vainly pursue the desert vapor - and wearied return, the dupe of their own imagination.'

Shahabudin Suhrawardi

'Show a man too many camel's bones, or show them to him too often, and he will not be able to recognize a camel when he comes across a live one.'

Miraza Ahsan of Tabriz

Reality is not only different from what we think it is, it is different from what we *can* think it is. As discussed, one of the principal understandings of the perennial psychology is that the ordinary person is subjected to social conditioning and cultural programming to the degree that they do not fully realize themselves. This is not meant as a criticism but as a sincere observation – and a very necessary one. Unless this awareness can be grasped, there is no hope in progressing upon a self-developmental path. This awareness is the very foundation upon which everything else is built. Just as one would not build a house upon sand, nor would one build the Self upon the false.

People have been conditioned to respect, and believe, in social authority figures. What would happen if one day a leading expert made a global announcement, supported by the United Nations, that it has now been affirmed that human beings have always been insane. How would you react to it? Moreover, how could *you* disprove this? How can any of us prove the species sanity? Everything people know, or believe they know, is based on relative comparisons. Human systems of knowledge are based on relative understanding. It was once consensual understanding that the earth was at the centre of the solar system and everything else revolved around this planet. It was also once thought that the earth was flat! We may laugh about these ideas now, yet they were taken seriously *in their time*. General knowledge is a subjective thing. It is based on relative truths – not on Reality. For this reason, it has been said that humanity is 'asleep;' occupied only with the transitory and fleeting things of the world. The Persian poet Hakim Sanai[i], in his work *The Walled Garden of Truth*, said that – 'If you yourself are upside down in reality, then your wisdom and faith are bound to be topsy-turvy.'

The perennial wisdom tradition recognizes that there are external influences and forces active in the world that seek to keep humanity 'asleep' and distracted from a life of inner development. Partly, this is the game. It is comparable to the children's game of hide-and-seek. The whole human race is like an organism, and within this organism there is disequilibrium. Because of this disunity it is not possible for the organism (humanity) to develop in the normal way. At the same time, there is something that infuses this organism and is responsible for its development. This component facilitates the possibility for a certain kind of development to what (for want of a better word) we may call a 'higher level.' The perennial psychology represents an aspect of this component. This potentiality allows for development to occur deliberately; that is, upon a conscious level rather

i Born in 1080 and died between 1131-1141

than by chance. For this reason, some have referred to this process as 'conscious evolution.'

In this regard it has been said that humanity has both an origin and a destiny. The Higher Knowledge deals with participation upon this path toward a known destiny. Until a person can know of their place within the cosmic scheme, they shall remain within the lesser state of relative and limited understanding. In past times, the genuine wisdom teachings were kept away from general circulation - away from the 'ordinary person' – and for good reason. It was considered inappropriate to expose unprepared people to such knowledge. Rather than helping, it would lead to imbalance, and personal as well as social difficulties. Long preparation was usually required before access to such wisdom teachings was allowed. This gave rise to what we know today as initiation periods and similar such lengthy preparatory processes. This has been necessary as an unprepared mind can be affected by fantasies of grandeur, superiority, or other such unhealthy traits that can cause harm, or unbalance at best. When a person is deemed 'mature' then there is no prohibition – higher knowledge is freely open to them. It has been, and always will be, a matter of capacity. This is neither arbitrary nor unjust. However, things have now changed. A different energy has entered the equation which makes long, preparatory phases now unnecessary, as I shall discuss in more detail later.

The perennial path is directional, not random. Its efforts are regenerative; that is, renewing the manifestation of perennial truths according to the time, place, and the people. Within each society, or culture, it is necessary that those who approach the perennial path have a stabilized secondary self. In other words, the conditioned self (or personality) is harmoniously integrated into the social milieu. This is the same whether it applies to a secular, religious, technological, or agrarian environment. A socially unbalanced aspirant may find that exposure to perennial impulses only confuses them in terms of social role or position in life. This can lead to emotionally exaggerated experiences, such as are more common with pseudo-spiritual gatherings or false 'cultural tribes.' People who are in need of therapy, social acceptance, friendship, or tribal togetherness, should seek out these experiences first before considering an approach to a genuine perennial path.

Social harmony is a normal requirement and state; it is not to be falsely equated with that of 'higher' experiences. Mental balance and the ability to fit into one's social environment are like essential nutrients and should not be confused with any show of higher ability. The first place to start from is a place of groundedness. Once this is achieved, then a person is able to begin recognizing the game for what it is. And what is the general narrative of this game?

The general storyline is that a person goes to school and is conditioned into obedience as well as accepting certain information as being 'accepted knowledge.' Lesser forms of this accepted knowledge are stratified into rote learning and examinations. Other forms of this programmed learning are coded into the specific local culture and broader society. These codes are often sanctified into norms, values, and other systems of social management. A person is expected to abide by these codes in order to gain and live a fulfilling life. Adherence to these consensus codes also allow a person to gain access to most of their social support infrastructure. To go against the codes – i.e., the programming – may result in ostracization, marginalization, criticism, oppression, or incarceration. A general line of this code says that a person needs to get a 'good job' to be a contributing member of society. This job should also economically support the system. We commit our lives to working in order to provide for the time when we are no longer employable – usually referred to as retirement. In these latter years of life people are then encouraged to find those pursuits that keep them comfortably occupied without, it is hoped, placing too much burden upon the social system. Eventually we die, and all remaining death taxes are paid. In other words, most people reach the end of life's journey without ever realizing that they have been upon a journey. As the writer Frank Herbert (author of the *Dune* series) once remarked - 'The mystery of life is not a problem to solve but a reality to experience.' However, experience upon this consensual storyline is incredibly limiting.

It is for this reason that many people seek for extra-curricular stimulation, such as in the form of entertainment, sports (including extreme sport), adventure, travel, or various forms of intoxication. In general, though, people are not encouraged to seek those experiences that may develop and extend inner perceptions further than society wants them to go. The individual, however, is allowed to pursue extreme external paths and is often actively encouraged to do so. Yet there is a noticeable absence of support for the seeker's path of internal self-development. And there is good reason for this. Knowledge gained through genuine insight and perennial gnosis provides a person with a perspective vis-à-vis their common reality not available for most people. This new perspective does not conform to the cultural conditioning that socially manages peoples' lives. Hence, a person must be prepared for this. Part of the initial stage of the seeker is to guard against the forces of discouragement. In this respect, one must be weary of the devil's tools:

Once the word spread that the devil was pulling out of his business and was arranging to sell-off all his tools of the trade to the highest bidder. The night of the sale all the tools were arranged for the bidders to view. What a motley crew it was! There were sinister tools of hatred, jealousy, envy, malice, treachery, plus all the other elements of evil. Yet besides these there also was an instrument that seemed harmless, a wedge-shaped instrument that appeared worn out, shabby, and yet was priced so much higher than all others. Someone asked the devil what the name of such a poor-looking instrument was.

'Discouragement,' answered the Devil.

'And why is the price so high for such a non-malicious sounding instrument? asked the bidder.

'Because,' spoke the Devil, 'this instrument is more useful to me than any other. I can enter the consciousness of a human being when all other ways fail me and once inside through the discouragement of that person, I can do whatever I please. The instrument is worn out because I use it almost everywhere and as very few people know about this I can continue to successfully achieve my goals.'

And as the price of discouragement was so very, very high even today it remains a tool in the property of the Devil.

There is a related saying that is relevant here:

'The devils are losing but have not yet lost. And the angels are winning but have not yet won.'

The modern seeker needs to be aware of the confusion and turmoil present in the outside world, yet at the same time has to be free from its negative influence. A genuine seeker is fiercely orientated to the positive in life. This is because they know, without a doubt, that the angels are winning – even if they have not yet won. And with this knowledge, they can play the game of life.

The Game of Life

It is hard to admit that life is something *other* than what we think it is. Because of the suffering and the pain that many people experience in life, it is even harder to consider that life can be called a game. Games are for play and fun – are they not? Yet the verb 'to game' also means to manipulate, influence, manoeuvre, or exploit a situation. It also means to try to turn the situation to one advantage or the other. Games are not only the fun type, they are also the strategic, intelligent, puzzle kind. Life is not a linear journey. Within its many twists and turns people often participate in manipulative and exploitative strategies (as well as lots of fun). This is usually how things get done – by getting 'one over' on others; by 'getting ahead' and all the rest. Life, in general, programs us to better ourselves by bettering others. And this then becomes incorrectly defined as social evolution, or the 'evolutionary edge.' This is a term that has been misapplied from a basic understanding of the narrative of natural evolution that has been taught and propagated. As such, people often feel vindicated to apply it to human social behaviour.

Yet it needs to be understood that these strategies are all forms of gameplay; as such, everyday life is a game. Like all games, it depends on how we choose to play it; and the rules we abide by. So, let's begin by stating at the offset that life is a game – and that the game is rigged. To be awake and aware is to admit that we are playing a game. And the aim of the game? The aim of the game for the aspirant/seeker is to participate and to be immersed in the game with full awareness of it. For it is the nature of the game itself to make all participants forget they are in a game. It is similar to entering a fog or cloud where previous visibility is taken away. Life is presented to us like a theatre play where all the actors on the stage do their best to convince the audience that it is all so real. As Shakespeare famously put it:

All the world's a stage,
And all the men and women merely players;
They have their exits and their entrances,
And one man in his time plays many parts
(As You Like It, Act II, Scene VII)

We each play our part – or parts – yet for most people it is unknowing participation. Notice how children immerse themselves in playing games. They are absorbed in their invented, make-believe worlds; sometimes populated with invisible friends. As adults we may laugh at this. They are 'only children!' we say to ourselves, not fully realizing that they are not so different from us. Many people also have fantasies - these are called ideologies, theories, hypotheses, truths and half-truths.

People convince themselves that this 'game' called life is actually something objectively real. And everything within our societies and cultures aim to persuade us in this. Yet there is still something deep within each person that senses that this is not quite right. Each of us may feel the pressure, the unspoken rule, that whatever we do, we should not give 'the game away.' Once the realization dawns that life is a game, then comes another responsibility – how to continue playing the game once it is known that it's a game? This is the paradoxical nature of awakening from the slumber within life. This is why so many fully realized people are often laughing. As discussed in Chapter Seven, humour is a major component upon the perennial path. Any half-decent seeker needs a good dose of humour. The more the fog lifts, the more that social and cultural conditionings become like a surreal joke. It's both funny and yet not so funny at the same time. Laughter sometimes is a healthy anecdote to the parody we find ourselves in.

The next question that arises to the awakening modern seeker is, how to find enjoyment whilst playing the game? Many people are subconsciously afraid of this notion of enjoyment. It is as if the human being has been conditioned not to truly enjoy satisfaction. To play the game and know it is a game can be a fascinating journey. Things can quite literally be seen in a different light. What we are ordinarily presented with, as part of the 'game rules,' is a world in black and white. This is like the famous checkerboard scenario where pieces are moved between the black and the white squares. This is the play of the game – the good vs. evil; the hot vs. cold, and all the rest of these dualities that form the basic game-fog. Part of playing-along-with-the-game is to pretend that these dualities are not part of the unity. That is, they are explicitly separate. And that life is composed of these separate parts being stitched together.

This game is played throughout all social institutions and is conditioned also through schooling and education. The first rule the system teaches us is that this game is not a game! Life is presented as if painting-by-numbers. Certain pieces, or segments, have a specific number and the person is told to paint – or colour-it-in – according to the number shown. So much of human life revolves around such similar number systems. Children are given grades at school which then follow them into higher education and, if they choose, further into university. University grades – or work apprenticeship results – then follow the young person into their career and are carried around for the rest of life. Social status is a graded form of compliance that psychologically marks people throughout life. These 'social grades' decide what clubs or cultural memberships people are allowed access to, which designate their social groupings. Membership clubs form a part of this participatory game; all the time adding to the illusionary 'reality' of the fog.

In a similar manner, it can be said that the 'game of life' is like a pack of cards. Each pack is divided into four classes (or suites) and within each class there is a hierarchy of numbers/status, finishing with the royal flush, including the ace. Each card (and/or figure) has its numerical value and its role. As each card game begins, the players decide upon the game rules. Each game has its rules and within each game the cards have their role and their function. The participating cards of the game are known; yet no-one can know just how the game will unfold. Yet there is one card that does not play by the rules and which always brings uncertainty – the joker. Every set of cards has a joker (or two!) in the pack. Sometimes these are taken out before the game begins so as not to disrupt the gameplay. The game does not know how to deal with the joker in the pack.

Likewise, social and cultural conditioning prefers a gameplay where the participants have known or fixed roles. Within this game, to 'find yourself' means fitting into a role that is socially acceptable. The game of life cannot tolerate non-participation. Within these rules people generally learn from others who tell them who they are. The problem with this is that the information on 'who we are' reflects the personality (the social persona) rather than the genuine self. This then strengthens the social personality which feeds the ego and 'fixes' the ego as a serious part of life. Individuals then seek to reinforce the personality rather than seeking for the essential self. In the end, people forget to seek for who they truly are.

This game of life is a game of the conditioned self where the main participant is the social persona that is driven by the ego. The ego generally wants simple questions and answers, which turn out to be meaningless. The ego is not seeking for the grander 'metaphysical' answers to life's questions, for such answers are inevitably contrary to its own dominance. The ego, along with the social personality, has a vested interest in winning in the game of life. The true self needs to be cunning here. The real question is how to play the game of life without giving the game away and also without losing.

The perennial psychology can assist in playing the game of life. It can assist a person in developing finer faculties of perception. When such faculties are cleansed, the person develops the capacity to perceive what may be called the 'metaphysical background' of the world. The perennial tradition of inner gnosis functions to allow a deeper knowledge of the metaphysical experience of the world and the person's relation to it. We may not be able to get out of the game completely, yet we can change our point of perspective, and hence our view of reality. This then completely alters the gameplay!

The person of today is called upon, in this struggle against the generalized oppressiveness of everyday life (i.e., the game), to nourish, strengthen, and enrich the luminous spark that is carried in the innermost being. Conscious awareness (cognition) is what determines the difference between people – not social or cultural markings. A person's level of consciousness, and hence perception, determines the ability to break away and act free from the automatisms of the world. This is playing the game – having the capacity to perceive and thus operate *beyond* the automatisms of the conditioned world. Intelligence and consciousness are two distinct things. A person can be seemingly intelligent and yet consciously asleep. For the majority of those participating in the game of life, certain inner faculties of the human being have atrophied; and they need to be awakened. This is the function of the genuine perennial tradition. A poem from Jalalludin Rumi states:

A man, never having seen water,
is thrown blindfolded into it,
and feels it.

When the bandage is removed,
he knows what it is.

Until then he only knew it by its effect.

In these terms, most people live and know reality through its secondary effects. Contemporary humans have been conditioned not to expand and express the interior realm outward upon the physical world. The result is that most people live isolated within the fleshy house of the body. For the metaphysician, this is like living an entire life within a dark room. Living a life cut off from the metaphysical background of reality is an existence where perceptual capacities are underused. Generally, there is no language, dialogue, or narrative in everyday life for understanding or articulating this deeper metaphysical background – a background that permeates the world. Human societies are undernourished in such matters.

Playing the game is about engaging in 'boundary thinning' between the consensus reality and the Greater Reality. The aspirant – the seeker – is one who attempts to reach out in order to catch the glimmers of a metaphysical reality beyond the ordinary everyday. And when they do so, something conscious touches them in return. The aspirant must learn to trust in such responses from the world. A form of feedback from an external impression can be like a thread that connects to essential things. A true seeker strives not to remain unused in life.

The modern seeker is no longer a preacher or a holy hermit living in a cave or some sanctuary away from life. Rather, the seeker of today is the perceptive person whose eyes are turned towards the presence of the Real. Such a person carries the intuitive conviction that they possess *within themselves* the resources they need -

> 'The Gnostic of today could no longer be a preacher of salvation, a holy man living a solitary existence on his mountain-top, nor some illuminated spirit living in a great city and devoting himself to his beloved ancient texts, but rather a perceptive man, his eyes turned towards the present and the future in the intuitive conviction that he possess above all within himself the keys to this future, a conviction he must hold steadfastly against all the reassuring mythologies, the so-called salvatory religions and disalienating

> ideologies which serve only to hinder his presence in the true reality. For the important thing today is not so much to discover new stars as to break down the new frontiers that constantly arise before us, or which are delineated within ourselves, so that we may cross over them, as into death, with our eyes wide open.'[1]

The modern seeker must live with conviction, and within society. The seeker can find within the things of the world all that they need to begin their destiny – if they are truly looking. The signs are there, deep within the world's dreaming. There are some things that the seeker is meant to find - certain things to be found and then brought back so that they may be given for others who are in need. This function has always existed like this, and so it will always continue to be.

The seeker is compelled to travel into the world with the deepest parts open in order to touch the metaphysical presence that permeates reality. The seeker must be prepared to be receptive to specific impacts that await. That is why a certain amount of deconditioning (or de-programming) is required. Otherwise these impacts will not be perceived, and the metaphysical background of the world will remain invisible to the seeker. Preparation is more necessary than protection. Protection is a response to fear, a built-up cultural myth against unknown enemies. Preparation is wise precaution that allows the unknown to operate effectively when it is met.

The seeker travels along the path of the perennial tradition not only for themselves but also for others. The seeker heals themselves so that they may become medicine for others. The seeker carries a medicine within them - in their energy, presence, behaviour, words and thoughts. The seeker allows certain energies to live through them so that those elements from 'beyond reality' can manifest in the world of today. This is the path that some of our human ancestors have taken for millennia.

Now we have arrived at the twenty-first century. The world of today appears as metaphysically undernourished. The general standard narrative lacks a coherent story for a thriving human future. The majority of humankind are busy trying to survive against hostile odds. The path of inner development is, unfortunately, a luxury for the few. Yet the truth is that we live within a deeper metaphysical reality – and the onus is upon the few to take up this call.

A new story is needed for the twenty-first century – a new understanding of what it means to be a modern person within a thriving world. The human species has entered upon a technological era of tremendous potential, as well as many possible dangers. The perennial psychology of today now reaches out to respond to a new time, a new place. The modern seeker is the aspirant of today. They too must understand the importance and the responsibility of the Work within a modern age.

References

[1] Lacarriere, Jacques. 1977. *The Gnostics*. London: Peter Owen, p128

Chapter Eleven

A MODERN AGE

'There is no epoch in history that seems to us as it must have to the people who lived through it. What we live through, in any age, is the effect on us of mass emotions and of social conditions from which it is almost impossible to detach ourselves. Often the mass emotions are those which seem the noblest, best and most beautiful. And yet, inside a year, five years, a decade, five decades, people will be asking, "How could they have believed that?"'

Doris Lessing - Prisons We Choose To Live Inside

Every age, every epoch, has its thinking patterns and modes of behaviour. Each age considers its knowledge to be superior to what has gone before. In each age people are under the effect of the incumbent conditioning and the mass emotions. It is not easy to detach from these influences, and the majority of people live their lives in obedience to them. It is useful in each age to be aware of those influences which are dominant and that are utilized to popular effect. The perennial psychology takes into account these dominant operative forces and functions in the knowledge of their presence and their likely impacts. The modern seeker in the world of today likewise needs to have a keen awareness of these foremost impacts and forces.

Within each era there are thought models or narratives that are popular. Often, they come as part of the social programming of each given epoch. That is, each era cultivates certain sets and parameters of thinking which are promoted and protected. These then filter down to influence how people's perceptions, beliefs, and thinking patterns are formed. People may have the 'belief' that they have free will, when this is in fact a delusion based on a perceived liberty of behaviour. Just as software programs the parameters and goal definitions of a machine, so does social conditioning program a set of codes into people and their cultures. Once these codes are known it can become fairly easy to predict the attitudes and behaviour of large groups of people. In general, humanity is much less individualized than its members believe themselves to be. The following tale illustrates how each epoch has its way of thinking. It is called 'Three Epochs' -

1 Conversation in the 5th century. "It is said that silk is spun by insects and does not grow on trees. And diamonds are hatched from eggs, I suppose? Pay no attention to such an obvious lie." "But there are surely many wonders in remote islands?" "It is this very craving for the abnormal which produces fantastic invention." "Yes, I suppose it is obvious when you think about it — that such things are all very well for the East, but could never take root in our logical and civilized society."

2 In the 6th century. "A man has come from the East, bringing some small live grubs." "Undoubtedly a charlatan of some kind, I suppose he says that they can cure toothache?" "No, rather more amusing. He says that they can 'spin silk.' He has brought them with terrible sufferings, from one Court to another, having obtained them at the risk of his very life." "This fellow has merely decided to exploit

a superstition which was old in my great-grandfather's time." "What shall we do with him, my Lord?" "Throw his infernal grubs into the fire, and beat him for his pains until he recants. These fellows are wondrously bold. They need showing that we're not all ignorant peasants here, willing to listen to any wanderer from the East."

3 In the 20th century: "You say that there is something in the East which we have not yet discovered here in the West? Everyone has been saying that for thousands of years. But in this century, we'll try anything: our minds are not closed. Now give me a demonstration. You have fifteen minutes before my next appointment. If you prefer to write it down, here's a half sheet of paper."[1]

We live in a modern age of great distraction as well as incredible promise. There is little doubt that these are indeed testing times. They are testing in regard to grasping what it fully means to be a human being – to be living a life as a conscious, human being. People are blinded to the many creative possibilities and capacities inherent within them. These capacities are dulled by a restrictive social and cultural environment that has become increasingly institutionalized and managed.

Living in a modern world places upon the individual other responsibilities. In part, these responsibilities have to do with finding a sense of one's self; and for one's inner life to develop in harmony with external demands. The individual requires a certain amount of independence in order to freely have self-expression. The suppression of self-expression, which is dominant in many cultures, often leads to dependency upon external institutions as well as certain indulgences, such as consumerism or distracting pursuits. These are often a way of escaping anxiety or depression which are emotional and mental responses to the suppression of a person's inner self. Many people have a sense that their creative capacities are underused, or that they are not given opportunities for full self-expression. The push toward further automated lifestyles, which is predominant in modern industrialized nations, is not conducive to the full self-expression of one's inner life. Within this environment, a person is compelled to find the necessary conditions that can allow them to be receptive to a developmental path. These are some of the obstacles that face a modern seeker in the world today.

It is imperative that any person seeking a developmental path have a deep sense of self-worth. Otherwise, it may be the case that what they are seeking is a substitute for their own lack of self-worth. This state is not only non-conducive to any real learning path but is detrimental to interior growth. Life in the modern era is accustomed to providing for a sense of lack. Modern societies promote the feeling or sense of lack in order to be able to provide a customized, consumptive lifestyle as a means of compensation. The sense of lacking self-worth leads to unhealthy behaviour and must be avoided at all costs. Self-worth is the individual's own measuring stick and can guide through the uncertainties that both life and the inner path throws up. At times, one's own self-worth is the only thing that lights the way forward. It must be nourished and cherished, and others forbidden from attempting to diminish it or take it away.

Although the modern era is characterized by mass communications and connections, there is a considerable absence in the concept of service. Within most societies, there is a lack in the understanding of service as a greater good. Service is often provided in terms of commercial care or paid assistance, yet not in human heart-cantered interactions. The perennial tradition stresses that human service is a fundamental part of the path. What the aspirant seeks for themselves must be found through what they can give back, both as an individual as well as part of the bigger picture. The developmental path is a reciprocal process, and perennial psychology has deep knowledge about what genuine universal service requires. Genuine service is only possible when a person has become individualized; that is, operating from the essential self rather than from cultural norms and expectations. Each culture has its own values on what it deems to be service. For example, acting out of a desire to feel generous or worthy is not true service as the person is participating in the hope of reward – in this case, to receive a sense of self-worth. A person must already have a balanced degree of self-worth in order to move ahead on a path of development. To move ahead by gaining emotional rewards upon the way will prove more detrimental than beneficial. Unfortunately, most modern cultures, in the western hemisphere at least, place high value and esteem upon such acts that generate emotional gratitude and social inclusion. In fact, there are many award ceremonies and glamorized spectacles that praise such 'socially worthy' actions. To any serious aspirant and seeker, these are but distractions upon the path. The perennial psychology rather views 'invisible service' as being the correct path.

One formulation of the function of service has been named as *adab*. This term has been used in the past to represent a code of conduct within some circles. The original root meaning of the term *adab* means 'to prepare a banquet; to invite to a meal.' It's more general and cultural meanings have come to represent politeness, courtesy, good manners, respect, correct behaviour, proper conduct, discipline, and service. *Adab* is courtesy, respect, and appropriateness. It is not formality but a code of conduct – of *being* – that adheres to the specific context in which a person operates. As it states, it is a respectful appropriateness. This implies that the individual is fully aware of their cultural surroundings and adjusts their conduct to apply to the situation. This could be in terms of relationship between friends, in relation to family members, in relation to the society and cultural milieu, etc. In some quarters, it has been referred to as 'beautiful action.'

There are many varied aspects to the concept of *adab* – conduct upon the Path – and they act as important guidelines to the seeker in any age. Such conduct is timeless, and is essential regardless of time, place, and culture. Some of these aspects may be described as the following:

* To make one's practices inwardly sincere, rather than outwardly apparent.

* To recognize one's own faults, rather than finding faults with others.

* To recognize one's own ego and to struggle against its overt manifestation by remembering that our greatest ally is Love.

* To limit one's preoccupation, worry, vanity and ambition over the world and the worldly.

* To seek to heal any wrong that may have been caused to another, and to correct any misunderstanding as soon as possible.

* To remember that no good will come out of the expression of anger or excessive amusement.

* To be patient with difficulties.

* To recognize and remember that all people are members of the same family.

* To avoid gossip and bad-mouthing.

* To be indifferent to favour or benefit for oneself. To show responsibility for receiving what is one's due.

* To be free of envy and ambition, including the desires to lead or instruct others.

* To do what one does in terms of genuine service - not for the desire for reward or the fear of punishment.

The perennial psychology is a system of great compassion, although seldom recognized for being so. This is because it does not engage in outward show or cultural forms of what are considered to be compassion or 'compassionate acts.' In general assessment, compassion is seen as sympathizing for the suffering of others. It is regarded as showing concern for the physical, emotional, and mental state of others and to act for their well-being. Compassion is therefore something that is shown – it is expressed and can be recognized as a virtue by observers. The perennial psychology functions in recognition of the well-being of others although does not necessarily express or manifest this publicly or in ways commonly recognized. This is partly because emotions are greatly manipulated within external environments. Societies and cultures have shown misplaced emphasis upon the evaluation, and conditioning, of various emotional behaviour and responses. Also, that to engage in culturally sanctioned modes of compassion, which may attract praise and recognition, can prove detrimental to the inner development of the individual.

The modern age, with its global media communications and overt commerciality and consumerism, specifically targets peoples' emotional states. Compassion has been exploited as another form to gain financial advantage. It must also be recognized that the perennial perspective operates within a broader scope than most people can realize, and its concerns are not only for the here and now. The lens through which modern society evaluates certain value sets is distinctly limited in terms of the perennial perspective. It would be advisable for the aspirant in today's world to be aware of these subjective value sets and how they are utilized (or manipulated) in various contexts.

The seeker will find it necessary to exercise great patience and flexibility when dealing with the everyday obstacles and chaos that life throws up. Modern life is one of bombardment in terms of impacts and stimuli. The environment of the human senses has become vastly crowded in recent years with an influx of electromagnetic energy, electronic sounds and noise, as well as high levels of deliberate misinformation and targeted messages. In a world of mass communication, we are constantly being told what we should want, or believe, or that we need certain things. The simple truth is that all people share a similar longing, a similar hunger, as this next story shows. It can be called 'The Story of the Grapes' –

Four travellers – a Persian, a Turk, an Arab, and a Greek – had agreed to travel together as companions for some time in order to share the road. They had spent the morning walking a great distance and had arrived at a village feeling very hungry. They found that they only had a small amount of money between them and had thus decided to use it to buy some food for them all. This had started them arguing over what food they should buy.

'I want to buy *angur*,' said the Persian.

'I want *uzum*,' said the Turk.

'We should buy *inab*,' said the Arab.

'No, we need to buy *stafil*,' said the Greek.

Another traveller who was passing by happened to be a linguist and he said to them, 'Give me your money and I will be able to buy food to satisfy all your desires.'

At first the group of four travellers were distrustful of the new traveller, yet finally they agreed to let him have their money to buy some food for them all. The man went to a fruit shop and bought four bunches of grapes which he returned to the group.

'This is my *augur*,' said the Persian.

‘And this is what we call *uzum*,’ said the Turk.

‘You’ve brought me *inab*,’ said the Arab.

‘No, this is what we call *stafil* in my language,’ said the Greek.

The grapes were equally eaten between the four travellers and they soon realized that their argument had been due to their lack of understanding in the language of the others.

The travellers are like the ordinary person in the world. The linguist is similar to a guide upon the perennial path. People recognize that they need something because of an inner hunger, yet they often give different names to this longing. Yet despite the different names attributed to it, it is the same thing. It may be called different names by religious institutions, or by philosophers or theorists. However, it is only when a person of knowledge appears (as in this case the linguist) that such hunger can be provided for with the correct nourishment. It can be said that people do not fully know what they need. Or they are unable to articulate their need due to a lack of self-knowledge or awareness.

Similarly, the perennial tradition is the wine made from the grapes. This longing for grapes represents the initial stage. The wine is not yet offered until the earlier stage has been absorbed and understood. This wine is the fruit of wisdom. The grapes are the earlier need for knowledge. Knowledge and wisdom are not the same, although modern society often confuses the two together. Likewise, modern life generally takes information to mean knowledge. Again, these are two distinct forms. Contemporary society has little understanding of wisdom. Although the word is familiar, yet few people can grasp what it really means. The modern age has steered away from the concept of essentialism. It prefers to view things in terms of relativity. Yet this shift into anti-essentialism is also a drift away from seeking meaning. Modern life (or 'post-modern' life) has a plurality of 'possible meanings' yet they lack depth. The perennial path identifies an ultimate Truth rather than a series of lesser truths that are relative. Because this Truth must be experienced to be understood, it cannot be adequately expressed in words.

The modern age places great faith and trust in words and language; that is, in external expressions. This perspective has resulted in the human mind developing to adapt to these strengths, whilst other functions have become atrophied. Any mechanism can only function for those uses it has been prepared for. This applies also for human cognition. People tend to take information and attempt to turn it into wisdom. That is partly why modern life is so bad at formulating the fundamental questions about who we are, where we are going, and what is the meaning of life. To process these questions the modern mind seeks to disentangle threads of information. It is largely unprepared for grasping insights of wisdom. It is for this reason, amongst others, that the modern seeker of truth will find themselves within the minority. This has always been the case.

The modern mind, to speak in general terms, has reached a functional level of stability, which is in-keeping with the overall stabilization of human societies. Yet at the same time, the human mind is underused in so many ways.

People have become accustomed, and largely satisfied, to deal with information rather than pushing further ahead to transmute this into knowledge and then wisdom. These are stages of a process and are not given or 'received' without due diligence, effort, and conscious intent. Within the last century, for example, there has been a shift from having black and white televisions to receiving broadcasts in colour. Current technology now boasts high-definition, plasma, and high-resolution pixel reproduction. This shift can be seen as an analogy with how human consciousness operates. The television broadcast was only received initially in black and white because of the lack of sensitivity of the TV (our minds). This black and white transmission may be equated with information. By developing the sensitivity and capacity of the receiver (i.e., the human being), then the broadcast can be received in full colour – this may be called as knowledge. To transmute this colour definition into 'high-definition' requires an extra level of technology (i.e., a 'developmental technology'), which can be referred to as the transformation of knowledge into wisdom.

The modern age tends to deal with this question of capacity by activating two general responses: i) to develop the intellect – this also includes pushing the technological side; and ii) to play with emotions and emotionalism. The effects of these strategies are that: i) there is a vast increase in the accumulation of information and data. This data collection lacks purpose and meaning and further isolates human society; and ii) emotionalism becomes further exploited and manipulated through media, propaganda, and popular distractions.

Both these responses lack any understanding of purpose and meaning, which is fast becoming a feature of the modern era. This is one of the reasons why the perennial psychology – as a modern expression of the perennial tradition – is so important at this time. There is a great need for the developmental path to be operative within the modern world. The idea of gnosis (direct experience) and of transcendence (inner development) have become discarded in recent times in favour of materialism and material consumption. The modern dominant paradigm is one that strives to construct an artificial world that is self-enclosing – a reality that has no place for the metaphysical or the intangible (the non-material). The dilemma for the seeker of today is that modern life lacks awareness of the metaphysical. Life has become like a hall of mirrors, each reflecting a viewpoint, a perspective, a hypothesis, that is vying for attention and control. It could be said that the modern age has attempted to excommunicate the presence of the esoteric, the science of wisdom. Yet the inner vision, the perennial Truth, can never be extinguished - only eclipsed. Now, within this barren landscape, it may be that the perennial tradition is finding greater need amongst people. The perennial psychology answers this need by presenting the ancient science of wisdom in a context and language appropriate for the times.

It can be stated that in each historical age, those working within the perennial tradition have made knowledge of the developmental path available to society in general. This knowledge has served to assist social advancement and cultural development, whether through institutions, organizations, academies, or projects. This is an example of how the practical use of external systems and groupings can be utilized for the transmission of higher knowledge. At the same time, the deeper wisdom has always been made available to the few who showed the capacity to receive. The modern seeker can find what they are in need of within all times and places – if they know *how* to look. In the modern age, there are new currents to attend to upon the seeker's path.

References

[1] Shah, Idries. 1995. *The Magic Monastery*. London: The Octagon Press, p25

Chapter Twelve

NEW CURRENTS

'When you arrive at the sea, you do not talk of the tributary.'
Hakim Sanai, The Walled Garden of Truth

'The people of the world have a fixed destiny.
But the spiritually developed receive what is "not" in their destiny.'
Abu'l Hasan Khirqani

The modern age can seem to many like an enormous bewilderment. It can be disquieting at the same time as being incredibly connected. Few people will doubt that a new phase of human civilization has begun. It is true to say that the same was said at the beginning of all the new eras, although it is more difficult to have perspective during one's lifetime. Hindsight is generally a stronger perspective than foresight amongst humans. Yet today there is a grand difference. And that is, humanity is connected across the globe like never before. This makes a lot of difference, for now human life is no longer only a singular affair. What happens in one part of the world now has a ripple effect in so many distant lands. A drought and food crop devastation in one far-off country will affect the supermarket shelves in another country. People are now realizing that they, and the world, are interconnected and interrelated like never before.

This interconnectedness has always been known amongst the perennial traditions. However, it operated more through an intangible sphere of consciousness. External connectivity has always been a more formal, structural medium. Yet the power of thought - of intention, focused imagination, and visualization – have always been functional modes of action-at-a-distance. In current times, the world is experiencing a rapid acceleration in its technological systems. However, it is recognized that the connections of the modern world are mostly external connections. There is still little focus upon the internal threads that connect together the human individual and collective spirit. The modern era is now opening up a whole wave of new currents. A multitude of choices, opportunities, and resources are being made available. Those areas or subjects once considered fringe or alternative – such as the esoteric realm – are beginning to be more openly accepted into modern culture. As noted previously, much occult knowledge was kept away from open view (hence the term 'occult'). A long preparatory period was required before the aspirant could be given access to such information. This mode of operation has now shifted. Due to a distinct advancement in general human cognition, much information that was previously occult is now on open display and seeded through many channels of popular culture.

There are great benefits to be had from these changes, as people can more freely engage in pursuits of inner development without fear of persecution (as previously may have been the case). At the same time, new challenges face the aspirant who chooses the perennial path. These new challenges constitute the social and cultural context that shape the person's ambient environment – physically as well as mentally and emotionally. As discussed in previous chapters, each individual grows up amidst an array of conditionings that shape the personality. In today's age, such impacts as programming, propaganda, and mental control (brainwashing), are more widely dispersed through technological systems. These constitute, especially, dominant cultural memes and suppressing narratives. The stories we tell ourselves are now more powerful than ever.

Humans have always lived by stories more than by facts. Often, the simpler the story the more adherents it receives. This is why myth is so powerful. And this is also why 'mythical packages' have had such a powerful, and at times devastating, effect upon the development of human society and culture. These range from religious-spiritual stories to ideologies, theories, hypotheses, and ideas. Whether the world is flat, the Earth is the centre of the universe, or fascism as a utopian ideal – they all serve to capture, and steer, the human imagination. Humans have been so good at controlling the world because they have been so good at not only sharing stories but, more importantly, in persuading others to believe in the same story. Many people share the same dreams because they have been brought-up (weaned) on similar myths and narratives. On a positive note, this can lead to cooperation and collaboration. However, it can, and often has, also led to great struggle, conflict, and loss of life. Because of the great reliance upon stories and human-constructed myths and narratives, humanity is now not particularly adept at recognizing the difference between fiction and reality. In most cases, people invest in stories to make them *real*, regardless of whether they hold any truth or not. This is how humans have created meaning for themselves – by investing in stories that have provided them with suitable, and sometimes comfortable, answers. The problem today, however, is that many of these stories are now collapsing. The world, and the greater universe, has become simultaneously more awesome as well as more bewildering.

The question that faces many people today is how to live and engage with this bewilderment when there is so much uncertainty and rising insecurity in the world. The old stories and narratives are no longer functioning. They are not able to explain the world, the cosmos, or humanity's place in it. The modern trick has been to pump up the conditioning in place of presenting more meaning. The result is that people are programmed into obedience rather than into genuine inquiry or seeking. Obedience may be a contemporary form of dealing with increased uncertainty in life, yet it does not prepare anyone for dealing with the arrival of new currents – the new narratives and stories that will eventually emerge to replace the fading of the old ones. The opening decades of the twenty-first century represent a significant time. They mark a shift between eras. As such, they will show future historians the era where the old models were broken from and where the new stories began to emerge. The gods of old were replaced with a new understanding of reality and of humanity's place within it. Yet the road of transition will be seen to have been rocky.

For these reasons, amongst others, it is both an important as well as a difficult time to be an aspirant, a seeker after Truth. Important because it is crucial that the forces of materialism, over-rationalism (sometimes manifested as madness), and control, do not oppress the expression of the human spirit. And difficult because of these very same factors. The perennial tradition has existed within the vehicle, or form, of religions and/or 'spiritual' bodies in the past. This was a necessary, and functional, way to operate that was fully conducive with the times. These times have now changed. A religious and/or 'spiritual expression' may now not be the most appropriate form to adopt. The perennial spiritual science – the developmental path – can now be expressed through psychological terms thanks in large part to new scientific knowledge of the human mind, which has also provided a popular vocabulary in these areas. This psychological focus is also appropriate to the contemporary times. By this, I refer to the emerging, and accelerating, modern technologies. As the physical world becomes increasingly automated, data-organized, and socially managed, it will be ever more necessary to develop psychological well-being and a human sense of meaning and self-worth.

Present day historians are already discussing how by the middle of this century there will have been so many accelerating changes that many traditional models will be obsolete. Social and cultural systems will need to adapt quickly in order to provide stability for people. It is hard to say just exactly how the future will unfold. Yet with the rapid developments in information and biological technologies, life as it has been known will enter profound transformation. Within this unfolding, however, one thing remains constant – True Reality. Reality beyond external forms is a not a transitory phenomenon. The Truth has no form. Yet the means through which people perceive Truth has forms. As such, forms are limited; they generally operate according to the time, the place, and the culture. Forms belong to the external world; as such, they obey a shifting environment and a changing context. Forms act as a vehicle, an instrument, and so they also outlive their usefulness. Whilst most people adhere in obedience to the external form, the sensitive person is urged to seek beyond this. As such, the seeker's role remains as it always has. Only now, that the Path one needs to take is through an altogether different, and sometimes beguiling, environment.

People have always sought meaning from within their social and cultural environments. In past eras, people revolted against oppression and tyranny, for example. This overt struggle created meaning and purpose. Often it was for obtaining improved living standards and for well-being. In the future, these struggles are likely to be replaced by a new necessity – to find relevancy within the world. This existential question is likely to raise its head again – how to struggle against the loss of personal meaning? The upcoming years, and decades, will be characterized by a crisis of soul-searching. That is, more and more people will be compelled to find answers for the role and function of the human being. Part of this push will come from the increased integration of advanced technologies into human life.

The human species is not a separate being, despite the many stories telling it is so. In recent centuries humanity has become divorced from the natural world, its natural habitat. Humanity has come to view itself as 'struggling' against Nature in a bid to conquer and control it. Much energy has been spent trying to wrestle Nature's secrets from her, according to empirical science. The human species has woven its stories of being a special species above and beyond others. Humanity created the myth that it is the lone species and unique amongst the universe. These myths and this mythmaking have estranged humanity and taken it into polarity. This is contrary to the higher knowledge of interconnectedness between all living beings and the planet. This narrative of separateness and polarity now dominates how humanity sees itself, the universe, and its place within the grand scheme of things. These are all hindrances upon the path of inner development. These conditionings need to be put aside in order to allow new perceptions to grow and develop within the modern human.

In recent history, humanity shifted from an agrarian civilization into a socialized one. This included, for many societies but not all, a further shift into a stage of industrialization. By all accounts, human civilization is now globally shifting into a technological era where automation, algorithms, and smart software will increasingly come to regulate and organize modern life. The older generations are weary of this; many are fearful of it, as is natural. The younger generations, many of whom were born into a digital world, find this prospect encouraging and positive. Whatever the outcome – and there are many possible outcomes, some more desirable than others – the meaning of existence will fall onto the individual. Each person will be called upon to seek for relevancy. And for many it will not be easy. Many will need to leave their illusions behind.

From now, and into the years ahead, each person will be compelled to know themselves better. This will include such lofty questions as first expressed in the early part of this book – who are we? What do we wish from life? How can I give my life meaning?

As human life becomes increasingly automated, each person will be sharing more data, expressing their 'selves' online, and distributing their personalities through an array of gadgets, devices, systems, and networks. The human 'being' will seem to be a distributed and decentralized presence. This *persona*, however, is not the essence of a person. It is an aspect of a person that will function as part of their social environments and cultural milieu. This 'sense of self' will participate in the shifting world around it. Yet at its core, it will feel it is missing something. This something is the knowledge, understanding, and experience of unity and unification. This can also be said to be an expression of the genuine human heart. Not the sentimental love found in movies and pop songs; but the true bonding of the human spirit through energetic resonance.

The perennial psychology is a body of wisdom that can assist in preparing an individual to approach one's own experiential knowing of this unification energy – the Source. This path offers an accelerated trajectory of growth; left unattended it may take an unknowable period of time. A time that is well outside and far beyond the years of an individual's lifetime. Yet there exists the possibility to engage in a conscious and directed effort toward this goal.

It is said that the present era represents a completely new phase in human evolution, in that for the past ten thousand years humanity has had the possibility for conscious evolution. That is, evolution for humanity can move ahead through deliberate, conscious, directed effort. We can participate as individuals to achieve that which is not in our original destiny (to refer to Abu'l Hasan Khirqani's opening quote). And this is part of the ongoing living work.

Chapter Thirteen

THE LIVING WORK

'The consciousness of the 'work' resides within the whole community...a community of people who act as a sort of electrical battery which accumulates and discharges a certain sort of energy essential for human progress. This progress, however, is evolutionary: it leads towards the growth of a higher form of man. All other human enterprises are less important; sometimes these other enterprises (some of which we prize so much, as nations, cultural groupings and so on) have to be attenuated because they are producing a force hostile to real human growth.'

O.M. Burke

'A number of people working, thinking, feeling and offering themselves together with each one consciously involving his or her essential being,are capable of producing a thing of amazing beauty.'

Omar Ali-Shah

The perennial psychology is a living tradition. It lives through people and flows like a thread of energy. It is a living vibration and is connected at all times with Source. What it seeks is to manifest through the lives of people – and for this living energy to be transmitted into the world. People can choose to do a thousand things in their lives, yet if they are not true to their essential self they will have achieved little. This is what Rumi was speaking about in the opening quote from Chapter One. We are all connected, with one another and with the world round us; and this is our responsibility. The true inner path also leads through life. The seeker is both the walker and the path. There is no separation, no division or polarity. It is us – the human being - who creates the separation and creates the splintered mind. As within, so without – as without, so within.

Humanity is shifting into a planetary civilization as modern technologies reach out across the globe. And yet humanity remains fractured as a species. The human being has access to a collective consciousness and yet it is only known of as the collective *unconscious*[i]. This is not good enough – we can do better. We *must* do better. Internally, the human being is more connected than any technology could ever achieve. Technology may be a social mark of the epoch and stage of material development, yet the true mark will come from the state of humanity. Each person has their lives, obligations, struggles and setbacks. Yet everything that a person does, matters. Nothing is lost, even though it may seemingly go unnoticed. Everything matters.

Every person is here to learn; each in their own ways. To understand this requires humility. It also requires patience. It is not a question of passivity. It is a question of correct participation. As Buckminster Fuller eloquently put it - *'We're like bees you see, bees that go out looking for honey without realizing that we're also performing cross-pollination.'* As people go out about their business, *our* business is that of cross-pollination. It occurs even if the individual is not aware of it. How much more satisfying to know that a person could be a conscious part of it?

i As put forth in the research and writings of Carl Gustav Jung.

For the living energy to flow, humankind needs to allow and facilitate this flow. At times, this means getting out the way so as not to become the blockage. Knowing when to *step into* and when to *step aside* is also a part of the perennial psychology. It is important to get back to the essentials. If there ever was a time for returning to the essential, that time is definitely now. As a species, humanity has lost touch with the vibrational harmony of its home planet, Earth. There are those who continue to go about their daily lives within the old structures of division, polarity, and separation. These are thought patterns of conflict and conquest. Some people may think that they have conquered the world, but it is not so. A small minority continue to believe that they can win through conquering – but they cannot. It is a dying pattern, and its time has come.

The living work is an energy and presence of harmony. The perennial path is to be 'in the world yet not of the world' and this means harmony and unity. The opposite of this means separation and division. Where there is division there is no connection with the essential. Humanity has entered a period now where it is essential for reconnection. We each have a responsibility to represent a living tradition of conscious beings. It is not time to be fake. The social world has a lot of fakery, and each person must be aware of this and tread carefully.

Things are going to have to change because this is the necessary path of evolution. Evolution for the planet, for human civilization, for communities, and for individuals. Human existence is like that of the famous matryoshka Russian doll, with layers upon layers. Each layer is a physical form in existence, and yet connecting all these various forms together is the energy of consciousness. This is the energy that binds, and which at its fundamental state is pure unity. Everything – life and non-life – is unified. What we call death is not an end point, an abrupt termination. Death is built into the system – it is not a glitch or anomaly. It is a way of transition and continuation. It also teaches that what is more important is how to live. At the middle of the paradox lies a straight line. The living perennial work operates concisely and completely within the midst of life. To live within the midst of life is where the exercise of the perennial path takes place. The Path expects the individual to live everything life brings as though it were an exercise, being fully present.

There is a tale of two seekers-of-truth who meet after many years. The first one had evolved and the other one hadn't. The latter asks the evolved one what he had done and if he had found a Teacher to help him. The other answered: 'I lived life as if it was an exercise.'

Great opportunities can be missed because of the smallest of inattentiveness. The exercises to be found amidst life may be missed because a person is sleeping. This is how the majority of life is now. When a person is not aware of presence and the inner state, then they can easily be drawn into conflict and into the mass collective psychosis that generally governs everyday events. The living work of the perennial path is about maintaining the positive at all times. This is because a negative thought interrupts the process of development. Even in adverse situations, the positive aspects must be sought out. The price of individual freedom is constant watchfulness. Being alive is to be alert. This alertness is not time-based - it is presence-based.

> A seeker once asked a Sage: 'How long will it take me to arrive at the point of true understanding?'

> The Sage answered: 'As soon as you get to the stage where you do not ask how long it will take.'

People are interested in many other things – time, attainment, enlightenment, miracles, and the rest - when they would do better to be interested in Truth.

Other people in life will often come and go, as each have their own paths – but the *you* will always stay. It makes all the difference that *you* don't abandon yourself. The living work lives through the human being; just as the varied threads woven together make the complete texture of the carpet. Each individual thread has its own integrity and quality; when placed together in a harmonious relation that integrity is magnified and multiplied. The thread does not lose its own character or personality. On the contrary, it willingly offers itself towards the production of a thing of utility and beauty. Likewise, each individual person too has within them the potential for a quality of being and a noble integrity. When people act together in harmony and cohesion they create an extra factor – an extra form of energy. It is the free choice of each person whether they choose to take on the responsibility of a conscious being working upon a developmental path for the benefit of both themselves and for the wider evolutionary process. This choice should be taken with joy, humility, and responsibility. The path of the Perennial Tradition can be walked with the confidence, quiet enthusiasm, and assurance that the essential being is awakening to a finer perception of higher knowledge, leading to Truth. The opening up of finer perceptions will call down the energy of inspiration as a guide. Within the distortion of the external world, such inspiration can be the sweetest fruit:

A person found themselves hanging off the side of a cliff. They had slipped yet managed to grab hold of a tiny shrub growing on the cliffside. There was no way for them to climb back up the sheer rock cliff face. Below them was a drop of a hundred meters onto the ragged rocks below. It was then they noticed a small bunch of berries growing not far from them. With their one free hand they managed to reach out and take a few berries. The roots of the shrub began to come loose from the rockface. With careful precision they placed these few berries into their mouth. How sweet was their taste!

This short book has been written with the intention of revealing some of the aspects of the Perennial Tradition. The perennial path is a long tradition, and it is never ended. It has many forms. Some of them are not known as a developmental path at all, so many people do not recognize it as such. Yet it has always been around. For as long as there are people in the world, so the path will continue to operate, in whatever form. It is a story that has always been recited within the hearts of humanity, and so it will always continue to be told.

Will you - the reader - find the story of the Path within your own hearts, and help the living work?

Epilogue

1. The human environment produces certain subtle changes in the individual which penetrate his whole being. Instead of undergoing only these changes, Man has a chance to gain access to a form of self which is, by comparison, infinitely superior. To use the technical term: he is at present 'only half awake.'

2. This change, although it increases Man's awareness of his destiny, does not interfere with his ordinary human relationships. On the contrary, it enriches them.

3. In order to take part in this process, there has to be the coincidence of a teacher with the doctrine, the application of the doctrine in a way suited to the pupils; and the right environmental circumstances. Nothing less than all these factors will do.

4. One way of rendering the message given here is that there is a deeper truth, and a wider dimension, in which Man already partly lives, though he is ordinarily indifferent to it. There is the hope that he can become as aware of it as he is of the familiar world.

5. The self-realisation of this dimension enables a man or woman to attain heights of achievement in the easily-perceptible world and in other areas; and prevents him from becoming the tool of a mere conditional existence, with all its anxieties and ultimate meaninglessness. Man tends to be unhappy not because of what he knows, but because of what he does not know.

6. It is only through the attunement of a group of people, each with the possibility of this attainment, correctly harmonised into a true community (whether physically in contact or otherwise) that true understanding and the next step in human progress can come.

7. The unity and integration of this group are essential to individual as well as collective success. In fact almost the only opportunity for Man to realise his individual importance is through the support of a group of suitable people.

8. This doctrine and the manner of its application have been known and propagated from time immemorial. They are, in fact, the property and destiny of Man. They link with a past in which this development was much more widely known, through a present where it has fallen into disuse except for a few, to a future in which The Great Work will be the entire legitimate goal of Mankind.

9. 'The New Man,' 'The Real Man,' 'The Perfected Man' are all terms used in different formulations, throughout the ages, for this activity, which has been called secret,' 'hidden' or 'initiatory' for reasons other than people realise.

(Taken from: Shah, I. 1996. *Learning How to Learn: Psychology and Spirituality the Sufi Way* London: Octagon Press, p292-3)

Recommended Reading

Barks, Coleman; Moyne, John (Trans). 1996. *The Essential Rumi.* San Francisco: HarperCollins.

Burke, O.M. 1993. *Among the Dervishes.* London: Octagon Press.

Dennis, Kingsley, L. 2013. *Breaking the Spell: An Exploration of Human Perception.* Winchester: O-Books.

Dennis, Kingsley, L. 2018 (3rd Edition). *Meeting Monroe: Conversations With a Man Who Came to Earth.* Beautiful Traitor Books.

Dick, Philip K. 2001 (1981). *VALIS*. London: Gollancz.

Halevi, Z'ev Ben Shimon. 1984. *The Work of the Kabbalist.* Bath: Gateway Books.

Hoeller, Stephan A. 2014. *The Gnostic Jung and the Seven Sermons to the Dead.* Wheaton, IL: Quest Books

Jamroz, Wes. 2015. *Shakespeare's Sequel to Rumi's Teaching.* Montreal, QC: Troubadour Publications.

Jamroz, Wes. 2019. *A Journey through Cosmic Consciousness.* Montreal, QC: Troubadour Publications.

Lacarriere, Jacques. 1977. *The Gnostics*. London: Peter Owen.

Lefort, Rafeal. 2015. *The Teachers of Gurdjieff*. CA: Malor Books.

Ornstein, Robert. 1996. *The Mind Field*. Cambridge, MA: Malor Books.

Sanai, Hakim. 1974. *The Walled Garden of Truth* (trans: D.L. Pendlebury). London: Octagon Press.

Scott, Ernest. 1985. *The People of the Secret*. London: Octagon Press.

Shah, Idries. 1994. *The Commanding Self*. London: Octagon Press.

Shah, Idries. 1996. *Learning How to Learn: Psychology and Spirituality the Sufi Way* London: Octagon Press

Versluis, Arthur. 2015. *Perennial Philosophy*. Michigan: New Cultures Press.

Watts, Alan. 2017. *Out of Your Mind: Tricksters, Interdependence, and the Cosmic Game of Hide-and-Seek*. Boulder, CO.

For contact, write to: dr.solomonjames@protonmail.com